TANTRA
UNVEILED

Also by Pandit Rajmani Tigunait, PhD

Books
The Secret of the Yoga Sutra: Samadhi Pada
The Practice of the Yoga Sutra: Sadhana Pada
The Pursuit of Power and Freedom: Katha Upanishad
Touched by Fire: The Ongoing Journey of a Spiritual Seeker
Lighting the Flame of Compassion
Inner Quest: Yoga's Answers to Life's Questions
The Himalayan Masters: A Living Tradition
Why We Fight: Practices for Lasting Peace
At the Eleventh Hour: The Biography of Swami Rama
Swami Rama of the Himalayas: His Life and Mission
Tantra Unveiled: Seducing the Forces of Matter and Spirit
Shakti: The Power in Tantra (A Scholarly Approach)
From Death to Birth: Understanding Karma and Reincarnation
The Power of Mantra and the Mystery of Initiation
Shakti Sadhana: Steps to Samadhi
  (A Translation of the Tripura Rahasya)
Seven Systems of Indian Philosophy

Audio & Video
The Spirit of the Vedas
The Spirit of the Upanishads
Pulsation of the Maha Kumbha Mela
In the Footsteps of the Sages
Living Tantra® Series

  Tantric Traditions and Techniques
  The Secret of Tantric Rituals
  Forbidden Tantra
  Tantra and Kundalini
  Sri Chakra: The Highest Tantric Practice
  Sri Vidya: The Embodiment of Tantra

TANTRA
UNVEILED
SEDUCING THE FORCES
OF MATTER & SPIRIT

PANDIT RAJMANI TIGUNAIT, PhD

HIMALAYAN
INSTITUTE®

HONESDALE, PENNSYLVANIA USA

Himalayan Institute
952 Bethany Turnpike
Honesdale, PA 18431

HimalayanInstitute.org

Printed and bound in India by Thomson Press India Ltd.

25 24 23 22 21 20 19 18   7 8 9 10 11

ISBN-13: 978-0-89389-158-9 (paper)

Library of Congress Cataloging-in-Publication Data
Tigunait, Rajmani, 1953-

    Tantra unveiled: seducing the forces
    of matter and spirit / Rajmani Tigunait.
            p. cm.
    ISBN 0-89389-158-4   (pbk.: alk. paper)
    1. Tantrism—Rituals. 2. Spiritual life—Tantrism I. Title
    BL 1283.852.T64 1999
    294.5'514—dc21   99-20108 CIP

∞ This paper meets the requirements of ANSI/NISO Z39-48-1992
(Permanence of Paper).

TO MY GURUDEVA,
SRI SWAMI RAMA

CONTENTS

OREWORD

In the late 1950s a missionary in West Africa persuaded two tribal chieftains to accompany him to the region's largest city. Never having been more than twenty miles from their village, the two were almost overwhelmed with unfamiliar sights and sounds. Man-made structures more than eight feet high were outside of their experience, so naturally they were astonished by the tall buildings. But having built their own dwellings, they easily understood that one story could be placed on another, and another on that. Similarly the missionary's jeep was the only vehicle they had ever seen so the traffic was dizzying—but there was nothing in the rush and roar of trucks and jitneys that collided with their view of reality.

The three men wended their way through the crowded streets to the city's main hotel, and while the missionary was checking the party in, his guests noticed a door opening in the opposite wall to reveal a metal grate in front of a tiny room. The man seated inside folded the grate back to admit four men, who then turned and faced the front. Next the seated man pulled the metal grate over the opening, and the door closed. A few minutes passed while the tribesmen continued to take in the sights of the lobby. Then the door to the tiny room opened again. The man seated inside again pulled back the metal grate and out stepped—not the four men who had entered, but two women and two little girls! What black art was this that had reduced healthy men to women and girls? Sickened and terrified, the two tribesmen made for the street, bent on reaching home and safety as quickly as possible. The missionary raced after them, and once he understood what the problem was, he tried to explain what they had seen. But both men had witnessed the same awful metamorphosis and were not to be persuaded that they had seen something else.

It is the problem of "seeing" that lies at the center of the misunderstanding that swirls around tantra. Like the tribesmen watching the elevator, we cannot comprehend what we are seeing when we look at tantra until we enlarge our view of reality because the tantric vision is radically different from ours. Accomplished tantrics see the world and everything in it as an indivisible whole—as a tangible manifestation of the Divine Mother. This is not a metaphor for them, nor is it a philosophical premise; it is a living, breathing reality. Where we see duality—young and old, right and wrong, male and female, pure and impure—a tantric adept sees One. The Divine Mother is not in the world; She is the world. Indeed She is the entire universe, and to see any difference between the individual self and Her or between Her and any natural force or cosmic influence is misperception.

Most of us have heard this before, so there is a natural tendency to react to this information with a reflexive "I know," and resist it. But unless we can actually experience the world as a vibrant, seamless manifestation of the Divine Mother—if only for a moment—there is no meaningful way to "know" what the tantric masters see nor to understand what they do. As long as this unitary tantric vision of reality is a matter of intellectual understanding only it will continue to be misunderstood, misinterpreted, and misused. And if we take our dualistic vision of reality, paper it over with a simplistic philosophical formula ("Everything is sacred; nothing is profane.") presto! we have the exploitative sexual practices that have so sensationalized (and misrepresented) tantra in the West. This further complicates the challenge of "seeing" tantra—we have to be able to separate the popular view of tantra as an amalgam of black magic and sexual practices from the ancient and elegant philosophy of tantra that skillfully demonstrates how to use the objects of the world as a means for spiritual unfoldment.

The ancient view of tantra is veiled in mystery, and the only way to penetrate this veil is to patiently cultivate the ability to see the universe the way the tantric masters do. How is someone who is grounded—as we all are in the West—in a thoroughly dualistic view of the world to cultivate unitary vision? How do we see what we do not know how to see? The tantric vision springs from a variety of sources—knowledge of the scriptures, contact with tantric adepts, visits to tantric shrines, and a systematic course of disciplined practice, among others. The dilemma is that it is difficult to assimilate one in isolation from the rest.

So how to begin? As you will find in this book, translation of the scriptures is not the answer in itself. Few of the key scriptures are available in translation, and the accuracy and usefulness of the existing translations rest with the skill and understanding of the translator—which is impossible to discern without a subtle understanding of tantra. And even if you do stumble upon a good translation you will not be able to glean practices from it, for it is an inviolable principle among the adepts that none of the more potent practices is ever set down in its entirety. A crucial piece is always missing, one that can be supplied only by a master who will consent to teach it only to a fully qualified aspirant.

So leaving aside for a moment the all-important question of how to become a qualified student, how is one to find a master? As we will see in chapter two, one time-honored way is to make a pilgrimage to places where they are likely to be found—the famous shrine to the Divine Mother at Kamakhya, for example. Unless we *know what to look for, however, all we may find in the hills of Kamakhya are animals being sacrificed and an occasional group of seemingly intoxicated people. Or worse, we may find ourselves attracted to the practitioners of black magic and sorcery (who are often to be found at such places) because they match our illusion of how a tantric master looks and acts.*

Prepared students will have few such illusions—which brings us back to the question of preparation. As with all forms of yoga, the key is practice. But which practices and where to find them? One solution is to resort to the scriptures with the conviction that even an incomplete practice is better than no practice at all. But which scriptures? Without the skill to see beyond the apparent contradictions among various texts (many of which extol what they present as the method) it is impossible to select a practice and undertake it with the full faith and conviction necessary to see it through. For that we need a teacher. Without the ability to distinguish genuine from fake, a tantric practitioner from a tantric pretender, there is no way to begin to find our way from the realm of duality through the mist of misunderstanding that veils the true tantric vision from our eyes.

Obviously what is required is an entry point—a map of the territory and some clues about where to look, how to see, and how to soften our gaze so that the appearance of duality begins to melt away. This slender volume is that portal—a doorway to the experience of living tantra. If we are willing to put aside the notion that this is a task that can be accomplished in a month, or even in a month of months, we will find in these pages an understanding of the tantric vision, inspiration, and an open invitation to practice.

Deborah Willoughby
President, Himalayan International Institute

Chapter One

THE LIVING SCIENCE OF TANTRA

According to most spiritual traditions the desire for worldly pleasures is incompatible with the spiritual quest. You can have the treasures of this world, they say, or the treasures of the spiritual realm, but not both. This either/or approach sets off an endless internal struggle in those who are drawn to spiritual beliefs and practices but who have at the same time a natural urge to fulfill their worldly desires. This includes most of us. And when there is no way to reconcile these two impulses we fall prey to guilt and self-condemnation, or we repress either our spiritual desires or our worldly desires, or we try to have both, and become hypocrites.

The tantric approach to life avoids this painful and confusing dilemma by taking the whole person into account—our human as well as our spiritual nature. The literal meaning of *tantra* is "to weave, to expand, to spread," and according to tantric adepts, we can achieve true and everlasting fulfillment only when all the threads of the fabric of life are woven according to the pattern designated by nature. When we are born, life naturally forms itself around that pattern, but as we grow, ignorance, desire, attachment, fear, and false images of ourselves and others tangle and tear the threads.

Tantra *sadhana* (practice) reweaves the fabric of life and restores it to its original pattern. No other path of yoga is as systematic or as comprehensive. The profound practices of hatha yoga, pranayama, mudras, rituals, kundalini yoga, nada yoga, mantra, yantra, mandala, visualization of deities, alchemy, ayurveda, astrology, and hundreds of esoteric techniques for engendering worldly and spiritual prosperity blend perfectly within the tantric disciplines.

Tantric masters discovered long ago that success in both the outer world and the spiritual realm is possible only if we awaken our latent power, because any meaningful accomplishment, and especially the attainment of the ultimate spiritual goal, requires great strength and stamina. The key to success is *shakti*—the power of soul, the power of the divine force within. Everyone possesses an infinite (and indomitable) shakti, but for the most part it remains dormant. And those whose shakti is largely unawakened have neither the capacity to be successful in the world nor the capacity to enjoy worldly pleasures. Without access to our shakti, true spiritual illumination is not possible. Awakening and using shakti is the goal of tantra, and this is why tantra sadhana is also known as shakti sadhana.

Tantra is widely misunderstood, however. Many enthusiasts in both the West and the East mistakenly believe it to be the yoga of sex, black magic, witchcraft, seduction, and influencing the minds of others, a confusion that has arisen partly because tantra is a science as well as a spiritual path. As a spiritual path it emphasizes purification of the mind and heart and the cultivation of a spiritually illuminating philosophy of life. As a science, however, it experiments with techniques whose effectiveness depends on the precise application of mantra and yantra, ritual use of specific materials, performance of tantric mudras, and accompanying mental exercises. Such practices can be thought of as tantric formulas—they will yield a result if properly applied, regardless of the character, spiritual understanding, or intention of the practitioner. And when this scientific aspect of tantra falls into the hands of charlatans it is inevitably misused, giving tantra a bad name in the East and sensationalizing it in the West. It is not hard to find people who have learned to use a few tantric formulas to startling effect. It is far more difficult to find genuine tantric masters and authentic scriptures to undercut such distorted notions. Difficult, but fortunately not impossible: genuine masters and scriptures do exist, and by gaining access to them it becomes possible to cultivate an understanding of this com-plicated path in all its richness.

MY OWN QUEST

I was first drawn to tantra as a child when I heard about a phenomenon that had taken place in our village several years earlier. My father and his forefathers were *raja purohita*, the spiritual guides to the royal family of the state of Amargarh in North India. For generations the palace had been attended by tantric adepts who were staunch worshippers and devotees of Shakti (the Divine Mother), and until shortly before I was born they included twenty-four pandits and tantrics, headed by my father.

One day a saint from the Kabira order arrived at the palace, and the eldest prince and his admirers fell under his influence. As a result they turned antagonistic toward the tantrics and their practices, and in time their animosity came to focus on one highly advanced practitioner who worshipped the Divine Mother in a palatial Shakti temple. His ritual worship was purely tantric and centered around the offering of liquor, meat, fish—and probably sex, although my father never mentioned it. According to Hindu belief these ingredients are impure and therefore prohibited, so the group around the eldest prince watched the adept constantly and criticized him mercilessly. "He is creating an impure environment in the palace," they would say. "How can anyone justify indulgence and orgies as spiritual practices? It is total nonsense. We should inform the king."

Eventually they did, and the tantric was called to the court to explain his actions. He said, "I do not indulge in liquor, but I worship the Divine Mother with *bindu* ['the drop'], as prescribed in the scriptures and taught by my master."

Attempting to pin him down, someone asked, "Then why do you lock the door of the temple when you do your so-called worship?"

"According to the tradition, the practice I do must be secret," the tantric replied. "Only initiates can participate in this worship. At all other times the door is open to anyone."

The king found this explanation acceptable and the assembly was adjourned. But the zealots did not give up. They kept an eye on this adept and discovered where he got liquor and when he brought it into the temple. They knew the exact time he began his secret worship, and armed with this information, the prince and his followers invaded the temple precinct one night during the worship and pounded on the door to the inner chamber, demanding to be admitted. Caught in the middle of the ritual and unable to complete it properly, the tantric adept prayed to be forgiven for concluding the practice inappropriately, adding, "Mother, I am your child. Do as you wish."

He then opened the door and the group rushed in, only to find milk in the chalices instead of liquor, and vegetarian dishes in place of meat and fish. They stormed out in frustration. "The Divine Mother went out of her way to protect me," the tantric thought when they were gone. "What good is this place in which She has to go through such trouble?"

Early the next morning he resigned from the service of the king, as did several of the other tantric pandits; those who remained became apathetic. Before long a series of calamities began—fatal accidents befell the royal family, and diseases and disputes arose among them. Sections of the newly built palace collapsed one at a time, and the section of the palace that remained standing was infested with rats and snakes and overrun by pigeons. Within a few years the family's wealth mysteriously disappeared.

I was not yet born when the incident in the temple took place, but I vividly remember the run-down condition of the palace and the misery of the remaining members of the royal family. I found the story of how this came about so intriguing that on several occasions I asked my father, "How do these tantric masters become so powerful? What is tantra?"

He usually ignored my questions, and when he did reply his answer was always brief: "Tantra means worshipping the Divine Mother. Tantrics are her blessed children. Whatever they have is by grace of the Divine Mother."

This answer was so unsatisfying that it spurred me on to explore the mystery of tantra, and I grew up the fascinated witness of numerous simple tantric practices common in our village. For example there were villagers who lacked a profound knowledge of philosophy or spirituality but had extraordinary healing powers. I observed that some of them could neutralize the effect of a cobra bite by using tantric mantras (a practice still common in villages today). The instant they heard that someone had been bitten by a cobra they would drop everything and rush to the victim's aid—and because they considered it their duty to do this, they never

accepted anything in return. Then there were the *malis*, a
group of villagers who knew a ritual involving certain herbs
which gave them the ability to cure smallpox. Like those who
could heal snakebites, these malis felt morally obligated to
come to the aid of those infected by smallpox, and by restoring harmony in the atmosphere through their practices, they
arrested the spread of the disease.

Another phenomenon centered around a metal bowl,
belonging to an old tantric, which could be used to identify
thieves. The technique was simple: when an object was stolen
the villagers would gather, and the bowl would be passed
around; when it reached the thief it became so hot that it
blistered his hand. Similarly another metal bowl, this one
belonging to a man who was not even recognized as a tantric
practitioner, likewise helped to find stolen objects. Its owner
regarded it as a living entity and worshipped the power contained in it. If something was stolen he invoked the force of
that bowl, and it would float through the air to the place
where the stolen object was hidden; if it was buried, the bowl
would spin on the ground above the spot. This man was
admired by everyone but thieves.

Years later, when I joined the university, first in Banaras
and later in Allahabad, I had the opportunity to meet tantrics
of such stature that my mind still cannot comprehend them.
Among them were Swami Sadananda, Bhagawan Ram
Aughar, Pramath Nath Avadhut, Damaru Wale Baba, Bhuta
Baba, and Datia Wale Swami, to name only a few. These masters were not interested in performing miracles, yet miracles
manifested through them as sparks emerge from a flame. For
example snakes, monkeys, leopards, and other wild beasts
followed Damaru Wale Baba as he walked in the jungles of
Assam. And whenever he made a special offering called
shiva bali during a special tantric group practice known as

chakra puja, a female jackal invariably materialized out of thin air to accept it. Datia Wale Swami, an adept of *bagalamukhi*, one of the most esoteric tantric paths, was able to immobilize bullets after they had been fired, a feat witnessed by hundreds of people in central India.

During my college years I became so absorbed in the study of logic, Western philosophy, and non-tantric schools of Indian philosophy that I began to doubt the miraculous path of tantra and the extraordinary feats that I had seen with my own eyes. My enchantment with the academic study of philosophy, which places exclusive emphasis on logic and pure reason, led me to believe that tantric phenomena were mere acts of magic. And a few years later, when I was initiated by my master, Sri Swami Rama (who himself represented the lineage of Shankaracharya), my skepticism about the value of rituals and the existence of a divinity outside myself (such as the one supposed to reside in shrines and temples) became even more entrenched. For a time I focused only on practices that could be validated scientifically and intellectually. But this period was short-lived, because I soon witnessed a series of "miracles" that reawakened my original belief in tantra.

One such event took place while I was with a group of Americans, visiting one of tantrism's most famous shrines, Jwala Mukhi, in the foothills of the Himalayas. It was the last day of a nine-day celebration called Nava Ratri, and there were tens of thousands of pilgrims in the vicinity. The line to the shrine was at least half a mile long and barely moving. The sun was hot, even by Indian standards. Understaffed and overwhelmed, the police managed the crowd by forcing it to snake through a maze to reduce the congestion.

By the time our group extricated itself from the main crowd in the bazaar and squeezed into line, we had already drunk all of our water, and I was worried that my companions, who were not accustomed to such heat, would collapse. While I was trying to decide what to do, an imposing gentleman approached me and said with authority, "You should go and ask the police. They will let you and the people with you go to the temple without following the line."

I did not see any police, so I said, "What police?"

"You people follow me," he replied, instructing me to tell the group to ignore everyone and follow him. Then he plunged ahead, shouting, "Hey, move! Let these people through!" And as he walked the crowd opened, giving us room to pass. I was so busy keeping our party together that I had no time to wonder why the crowd was parting so willingly in his presence.

As we neared the temple we finally saw the policemen, and our guide directed me to talk to them. By this time we realized that something mysterious was going on, so I tried to keep my eye on him while I was talking to the police. But even though other members of the group were watching him too, he disappeared before our eyes.

From that moment on, everyone around us appeared to be enchanted. When we arrived at the main hall the police and the temple authorities blocked the line, letting the pilgrims already inside the temple go out, and then inviting us to enter through the exit passage. And so in peace and privacy we paid our homage to the eternal flame, which has been flaring from the walls of that cave for untold ages.

Later when I told this story to some of the learned people associated with Jwala Mukhi they said, with unshakable conviction, that the gentleman was either Guru Gorakhnatha, an immortal sage who lives there, or one of the attendant forces of the Divine Mother. And when I asked my gurudeva (who always taught "look within and find within") if this was a mass hallucination or, if not, how something outside of me could

Sri Swami Rama

be so powerful and real, Swamiji replied, "Why can't the divinity that is inside you be outside you too? It is everywhere. Due to the age-long sadhana of the adepts, the divine force dwells in such places in a condensed, concentrated, and vibrant form.

"There is nothing like reality being within or without," Swamiji continued. "The wall between within and without is only for those who are ignorant. The awakened divinity within you helps you find the divinity outside you, and vice versa." This is the basis of tantra: *Yatha pindande, tatha brahmande*— Whatever is in the body is also in the universe.

Tantric sites—such as Kamakhya in Assam; the Chhinnamasta shrine in Bihar; Datia, Khajuraho, and Ujjain in Central India; Pashupati Nath in Nepal; and Kali Math, Sri Nagar, Bhairav Ghati, Tunganath, Kedarnath, and Chamunda Devi in the Indian Himalayas—are the living abodes of tantra. In these places (as we will see in chapter 2) it is still possible to meet adepts in whose presence we can experience the full spectrum of tantra—from tantra for healing scorpion stings, curing fever and psychosomatic diseases, and producing fire from the mouth, to tantra for cultivating our power of memory, awakening kundalini, having a direct vision of the chosen deity, developing clairvoyance, and attaining the highest spiritual illumination through the practice of yantras such as Kala Chakra and Sri Chakra.

THE WORLD OF TANTRA

The tantric literature is so vast that it is almost impossible to study it all, let alone practice a significant fraction of it—in fact it is said that it would take even a true adept a thousand lifetimes to practice all the tantric disciplines. The texts are written in Sanskrit (with the exception of approximately a thousand texts in Pali, Prakrita, Tibetan, Hindi, and Bengali) and represent the cumulative knowledge of masters over millennia. We will take a look at the three main schools of tantra and delve into the distinctions between the left-hand and right-hand paths of the kaula school in chapter 3, but for now what matters is to remember that all tantric texts and the techniques they describe have one characteristic in common: they adopt an integrative approach to sadhana, with the objective of making the best use of all possible resources, within and without.

Because their scope is all-encompassing, tantrics have always discarded conventional standards of morality, ethics, and purity whenever those standards were found to be obstacles to the process of personal growth and self-discovery, and this has set them apart from the religion into which they were born. Yet their liberal and scientific approach to personal fulfillment has prevented them from forming a tantric religion. Thus at a social level tantrism refers to a particular way of life, at a philosophical level it refers to shakti metaphysics, and at a spiritual level it consists of a set of techniques for gaining access to the multi-level forces within the human body and the cosmos.

According to tantrism there is a perfect equation between the universe (the macrocosm) and the human being (the microcosm). Through direct experience tantric masters throughout the ages have confirmed that the active and dormant forces in the universe correspond to the forces in the human body, and that the whole universe lies within each of us. And because tantrics hold the human being to be the pinnacle of creation, gaining complete knowledge of this interrelationship is considered the highest tantric endeavor. To this end they have experimented with the power of sound (mantra), form, color, and shape (yantra), and have documented their influence both on humans and on the different aspects of nature. They have studied the subtle properties of animals, herbs, and minerals, and have found ways of awakening the forces dormant within them to activate mantra, yantra, and the power of the mind. And in the process they have discovered how the energies of herbs, minerals, gems, planets, and constellations correspond to different parts of the human body. These findings ultimately resulted in tantric systems of yoga sadhana, medicine, astrology, and alchemy, which are well-documented in tantric texts and allied literature.

As its diversity shows, tantra approaches sadhana holistically, holding that to experience the beauty in the fabric of life we must weave together all of its torn and tangled threads. That is why most tantric practices consist of a range of disciplines involving the body, senses, breath, and mind, as well as the use of ritual objects, mantra recitation, silent meditation, visualization of deities, and meditation on a purely abstract, formless, divine being. The goal is to demolish the illusion that a wall stands between the individual and the divine, to correct the false impression that internal and external reality are mutually exclusive.

Fire is the center of all tantric rituals, both external and internal; the study of tantra cannot be fruitful without the esoteric knowledge of fire. It is fire that transforms the gross matter of the herbs and other ritual ingredients offered to it into subtle energy that can be recognized by the corresponding subtle forces residing in the psyche and its counterpart in the cosmos. And this process is governed and guided by the power of mantra, yantra, and *ishta deva* (a personal form of the impersonal divine being), as well as by our own faith. And that is why tantric rituals, accompanied by a fire offering and performed precisely, help the practitioner achieve the desired goal quickly and easily.

Still, this is no simple matter. Tantra is a complex science involving not only extensive scriptural knowledge but also guidance from a competent master, who can create a perfect structure for spiritual practice. A master well-versed in tantric scriptures knows how to determine the exact time and place for performing the ritual to ensure its maximum potency, and to this end he or she can initiate a student into the appropriate mantra along with its corresponding yantra. By looking into the practitioner's planetary placement in astrological charts, the adept can give precise instructions on how to use specific herbs, flowers, minerals, and grains as part of the fire offering. What is more, every practice is accompanied by a cluster of disciplines, which only a true adept can teach with precision. These ordinarily consist of *mudras* (hand gestures) and *nyasas* (techniques for synchronizing the different forces of the main and subordinate mantras in one's body); techniques for creating a harmonious balance between oneself and the forces of the cosmos; and techniques connecting oneself with the power of the mantra by means of intense visualization of the deity along with the recitation of a long set of mantras [known as *kavacha* (armor), *kilaka* (anchor), *hridaya* (heart), *patala* (flower petals), etc].

FORBIDDEN TANTRA

Finding a tantric master and preparing to undertake these disciplines is difficult, and attempting to learn from those who do not know them is useless and may even be injurious. Those who do know the practices rarely teach them because many of the practices, like scientific experiments, require a precise technique in order to yield results. And if the practitioner's intentions are not pure, some practices can be used for destructive and selfish purposes.

For example there are scriptures which can be classified as "applied tantric science," which contain formulas which ill-intentioned tantrics can use for *marana* (killing), *vashikarana* (seduction), *mohana* (manipulating the minds of others), *vidveshana* (creating animosity between two people), and other negative purposes. But even when the purpose of these practices is not negative, experimenting with them without the guidance of an adept is like playing with nuclear weapons. This is why the scriptures label them "forbidden tantra." To discourage misinformed and unprepared students from undertaking them, the adepts warn: "An aspirant should not even open and read the scriptures containing these practices (*prayoga shastra*) without the guidance of a master."

An experience that Sri Swami Rama shares in his book *Living with the Himalayan Masters* illustrates how "forbidden" practices not only can awaken an extraordinary force but also can materialize it regardless of an aspirant's intention or purity of heart. Swamiji's master, Sri Bengali Baba (Babaji), had an old handwritten scripture that he always carried with him. Once when Swamiji was a very young man Babaji showed him this book, instructing him never to open it without his permission. This of course aroused the young man's curiosity, and he resolved to read it at the earliest opportunity.

That opportunity came one day when master and disciple were traveling in northern India along the banks of the Ganga and stopped for the night at a place called Garh Mukteshwar. After Babaji went to sleep Swamiji quietly took the scripture and sat down to read it in the moonlight. Almost immediately he came across a mantra with a commentary that explained how to practice it and what the result would be. Swamiji did not want to waste time reading the rest of the scripture; he wanted to see what would happen—so he memorized the mantra and resolved to do the thousand recitations required, along with the auxiliary practices of mudras and nyasas. There were, however, two other auxiliary practices which Swamiji did not know how to do—the invocation and propitiation to Bhairava, and the drawing of a protective circle (*Lakshamana rekha*) around oneself—but in his enthusiasm he undertook the practice anyway. He had no idea what would happen—but, he rationalized, in any case there was no reason to be afraid, for he was a student of a great master, whose blessing would compensate for any errors he might make.

Just before dawn, as he was nearing the end of the practice, Swamiji opened his eyes and saw a gigantic, nude woman making a fire several yards from where he sat. Thinking he might be hallucinating, he closed his eyes. By this time he had completed almost 900 repetitions, and continued the practice. After a while he opened his eyes again—and this time he saw an even bigger man, also nude, walking toward the woman and her fire. Frightened, Swamiji quickly closed his eyes again. Next he heard the thunderous voice of the man demanding, "Have you cooked my food?" The woman answered, "You haven't brought me anything to cook." Swamiji opened his eyes and saw the giant standing next to the fire, glaring at Swamiji and gesturing in his direction. "Why don't you cook him?" he roared. Swamiji fainted from fright.

When he regained consciousness it was dawn, and his master was standing beside him. There was no trace of the two giants or their fire, but as soon as Swamiji remembered them, he fainted again. This happened several times, until finally his master kicked him in the rear and shouted, "Wake up! I hope you got the lesson."

Many years later Swamiji explained to me that the results of these practices can be so overwhelming that an unprepared student cannot handle their extraordinary force. That is why before imparting these "forbidden" techniques masters lead their students through a series of rigorous tests to ensure that each has purified his or her mind and heart and is interested in higher spiritual pursuits rather than in worldly power and pleasure. Those who pass are given the practices, and when they are completed successfully the aspirant discovers the dynamics underlying the extraordinary forces that establish and implement the laws governing matter and energy. And because they are intent on attaining wisdom, peace, and everlasting happiness, such aspirants use these practices to subdue the forces of ego, anger, hatred, desire, and attachment.

The practices of "forbidden" tantra may or may not result in inner illumination—enlightenment—but they do unveil the mystery of the life-force which manifests in numberless forms. And they can help us see through the forces of matter and mind and attain a glimpse of the radiant divine being who shines both inside and outside us. They can also help us subdue, conquer, or seduce the negative forces in our own being, and thereby help us attain freedom from the obstacles they create—disease, inertia, doubt, fear, the inability to reach the goal, the tendency to slide back once the goal is achieved, and a host of secondary impediments such as grief and moodiness, as well as mental and physical instability. Tantric masters impart these practices to their prepared students so they can overcome these obstacles quickly and prepare themselves for even higher practices.

THE HIGHEST FORM OF KNOWLEDGE

The highest tantric practices are the ten schools of *maha vidya* (the great knowledge), and among them Sri Vidya is the most complete and comprehensive. (The practices related to the other nine *maha vidyas* are subsumed, directly or indirectly, in Sri Vidya.)

The goal of Sri Vidya is to give the aspirant a direct experience of the primordial life-force, or shakti, that holds all the cells and molecules of the body in place. This life-force is endowed with intrinsic intelligence; its vibration animates all creation; all forms of energy and matter emerge from it. And because this shakti vibrates in all aspects of creation, there is a perfect synchronicity among all forms of life. By unveiling the mystery of this life-force, Sri Vidya adepts are able to understand the relationship between the different parts of the body, between the body and the mind, between humans and plants, and ultimately between the microcosm and the macrocosm.

When the adepts discovered how to access this shakti and the domain of matter and energy animated by it they were able to pinpoint the precise nature and characteristics of the forces governing our anatomy and physiology as well as all other aspects of nature. And to communicate this knowledge to those who had not had the direct experience, tantrics referred to these forces as "deities," explaining that any deity (force) that dwells within us also dwells outside us. The deity that governs the formation of the human fetus, for example, also governs the germination of a seed. By knowing the nature of the force that regulates the development of the fetus we can also know the nature of the force that regulates the sprouting of a seed, and vice versa. This is the basic premise underlying all tantric thinking.

The tantrics developed another method of communicating their knowledge: yantras, or diagrams that express a practice visually. Just as modern scientists have developed equations such as $E=mc^2$ to communicate their knowledge, so have the tantrics developed equations to communicate theirs—yantras are equations expressed in the language of geometry. There are hundreds of yantras, some simple, some extremely complex.

The most comprehensive of all is Sri Yantra (also called Sri Chakra), which contains the entire doctrine and practice of Sri Vidya.

INFINITE KNOWLEDGE

Adepts who have mastered Sri Vidya are the rarest and most mysterious tantric masters. Because they have become one with the life-force, they have no predictable personality. Just as the life-force assumes different roles in relation to different aspects of creation, these yogis take on different personas in response to different situations in the world around them. I saw this myself in the same year our group visited the temple at Jwala Mukhi. At that time we also visited a site in the northern tip of the Vindhya mountain range, known as Vindhya Vasani, to view a full solar eclipse. But for me the greatest attraction was Gerua Talab in the surrounding mountains, reputed to be a stronghold of tantra sadhana. It is also the spot where two adepts had recently left their bodies in a yogic manner, and we were eager to see whether other advanced yogis were still residing there.

When we arrived we found a simple and peaceful place—but as we gathered under a tree a bizarre-looking man clad in black approached us. His name was Bhuta Baba (Ghost Baba). Seating himself on a wooden cot, he asked us who we were and what had brought us there. His manner was abrupt, and his behavior crude. It was evident that he was trying to get rid of us. Bhuta Baba seemed to be quite learned, but when I translated a spiritual question or asked his guidance in locating the spot where the yogis had left their bodies he made fun of spirituality and mocked the process of birth and death. Our group, however, remained humbly persistent, and he gradually became a bit more agreeable. Then someone asked him, "What is the most important thing an aspirant must observe?"

Sri Chakra

"Food," he replied in Hindi as I translated. "You become what you eat."

"So you mean vegetarian food?"

He laughed. "You people are naive. See? If you eat chicken, you will think and behave like a chicken. If you eat beef, you will think and behave like a cow. But if you eat human flesh, you will think and behave like a human."

I hesitated to translate this, but he insisted. By this time I had realized he was a tantric adept belonging to an esoteric tradition. So before I translated his last sentence I told the group about the uniqueness of that tradition and the deliber-ately bizarre lifestyle that its followers adopt. I also reminded them of the unbelievable power and wisdom these adepts often acquire through their sadhana. Then I turned to Bhuta Baba and asked him to explain why human flesh is the best food. At this, his behavior changed abruptly. "It doesn't matter," he said kindly. "Tell me, what can I do for you?"

He then revealed a few fragments of his infinite knowl-edge, and every question we asked was answered to our full satisfaction. Finally someone asked, "To be successful in both worldly and spiritual endeavors we need a one-pointed and clear mind. Can you tell us how to develop concentration and retentive power?"

He got up and went away for a minute, returning with the Sri Chakra. Pointing at its second circuit, he said, "By meditating on this, one can gain the power of concentration."

The same person then asked, "Can you tell us how to meditate on this circuit?"

With a smile he said, "Do you want to know everything all at once? Keep something for another day."

From the ensuing conversation I learned that Bhuta Baba was indeed highly educated and was an initiate of a great adept, the late Bhagawan Ram of Banaras. This master was a living link in the long chain in the lineage of one of the most esoteric tantric traditions: *aughar,* also known as *aghora.* The masters of this tradition are known for their miraculous powers, which according to the scriptures come to them through their mystical knowledge of fire. They specialize in the practices related to the *manipura* chakra (the solar plexus), as well as *surya vijñana* (the spiritual aspect of the solar science).

The whole group, including myself, was spellbound by Bhuta Baba's discourse on why sound and light are the primordial forces of creation and how they relate to mantra and yantra. Quoting tantric scriptures, he explained that sound pollution is the deadliest form of pollution, for it contaminates the most subtle element of creation: space—the medium in which everything else exists. Further expounding on tantric metaphysics, he explained how sound pollution can be removed through the power of mantra and precise tantric rituals. I was overwhelmed to discover his knowledge of solar science, because he was also an adept in Sri Vidya, which is essentially *chandra vijñana* (the lunar science), and it is rare that the same adept would be master of both. Although the local people found him a little frightening, they sought his blessings when they were suffering from physical ailments and mental trauma, as well as when they were ensnared in family disputes. Like most tantric masters Bhuta Baba has many personae. He is an enlightened sage to some, a healer to others, and a crazy mendicant clad in dirty black to still others.

Bhuta Baba was not the first tantric master I had encountered. Years before I had been fortunate enough to be in the company of a saint named Swami Sadananda, who lived by the Ganga on the outskirts of Allahabad, and had come to understand that meditation, mantra, yantra, herbs, and rituals can awaken each other and that their combined energy can be

polarized to influence the forces within us or outside us—
provided we know the exact tantric method to awaken and
polarize them. Like Bhuta Baba, Swami Sadananda was
known for his healing powers and miraculous deeds. On more
than one occasion he fed thousands of people from a tiny store
of food, transformed Ganga water into ghee, turned welding
metal into silver, and, using ash from his fire pit, cured hundreds
of terminal illnesses. Even today people remember Swami
Sadananda for his extraordinary knowledge of botany,
alchemy, ayurveda, and astrology, which he blended in such a
way that all of these sciences took on tantric overtones.
Scientists and philosophers from the nearby University of
Allahabad, initially skeptical, were fascinated by his knowledge of the spiritual properties of plants (a subject unknown
outside tantric circles), and many of these academics became
his students when they observed the outcome of his practices.

I witnessed one example of Swami Sadananda's powers.
Two parties were in court. As is normal in the Indian judiciary
system, hearings were postponed repeatedly, so the case
lingered on for a long time. As the animosity between the
litigants intensified, one party came to Swami Sadananda and
requested his blessings for winning the case. He replied flatly,
"I don't have such blessings. I can teach you a special practice
that will make you invincible, but I can't guarantee that you
will defeat your opponent."

The man begged for the practice, and finally, Swami
Sadananda gave him *aparajita vidya* (the knowledge pertaining
to the Invincible One), as well as several complementary
practices and the way to arrange them around the main practice. He instructed the man to complete a specific course of
japa (repetitions of the mantra) while sitting under the canopy
of the aparajita plant (*Clitonia ternatea*). After the practice
was concluded Swami Sadananda guided the practitioner in

Swami Sadananda

the process of making a paste out of the root, stem, leaf, flower, and fruit of the plant, energizing the paste, and putting a dot of it on his forehead. Then he told the man to meet his opponent in court. "He will become your friend upon seeing you," Swami Sadanandji said. "He will drop the case voluntarily— but you must promise that you will treat him as your friend and not hold on to your animosity." On the first day of the hearing, before the parties entered the courtroom, they looked at each other and animosity vanished.

When I heard about this I asked Swamiji, "Since you have this knowledge, why don't you help others who are also in court?"

"I did it as an experiment to show you people that these sciences are valid," he replied. "But as far as the case is concerned, it is not fully resolved, only postponed. These men will have to work out their karma sooner or later. Nothing other than knowledge and non-attachment can burn the karmic seeds and destroy the animosity between these two once and for all."

These and other interactions with tantric masters, together with the study of the scriptures, helped me to realize that nothing is impossible for a tantric. I came to see that tantra is a highly refined and sophisticated science. It carries an overtone of mystery only for those who do not understand the interconnectedness of all aspects of creation, and I am convinced that humanity could benefit immensely from tantra if it were to be studied and practiced systematically. But because the knowledge contained in books is incomplete I also know that the missing links can be forged only by working under the guidance of a living master.

However, because tantric masters often lead mysterious lives it is hard to recognize them. Many who claim to be tantrics are not, and distinguishing an adept from a pretender is an accomplishment in itself. Making pilgrimage to tantric sites creates an opportunity to meet the adepts, but you must remember that these places are also occupied by charlatans, who earn their livelihood by hoodwinking the gullible. A comprehensive knowledge of the scriptures will help you distinguish a master from a pretender, and then you will be able to wholeheartedly commit yourself to practice under someone's guidance. The realization that you have found the right teacher will destroy your doubt and fear. As you follow his guidance the inner meaning of the scriptures and tantric sites naturally unfolds, and you will walk on the path with full confidence that the goal is within your reach.

Chapter Two

WHERE TANTRA STILL THRIVES

*J*antrics have never involved themselves in religion, either as advocates or critics, but the myriad techniques they have developed for enhancing the quality of worldly and spiritual life have proved so potent that tantrism has influenced every aspect of life, including religion, in India and neighboring countries. But tantrics themselves have shunned the spotlight, doing their practices quietly to avoid notice. Some have practiced at home, but the intricacy of the rituals and the long hours required to complete them make this difficult, so most have preferred to practice in secluded spots. The most suitable sites are remote, offering only the bare necessities, so that only those who are fully committed to sadhana are attracted to them. What is more, not satisfied that their austere environment would guarantee sufficient protection from the curious, tantrics have often deliberately adopted bizarre behavior and assumed a socially unacceptable appearance. For example Bhuta Baba dressed in dirty black garments and gave the impression that he ate human flesh, although he actually did not. Other tantrics at Gerua Talab carried human skulls, pretending to use them as bowls, in order to excite a sense of disgust and fear in visitors.

This behavior, intended to repel casual seekers, has always acted as a magnet to sincere *sadhakas* (spiritual aspirants), for here, in isolation, they have been free to experiment with tantric techniques that would have created a furor elsewhere. Thus in the course of time these remote sites became laboratories for tantra sadhana. Originally *mathas* (monasteries) or ashrams, over time the energy generated by the intense and prolonged practices conducted there became so concentrated that they came to be regarded as shrines. Disciples and followers erected monuments in honor of their masters, or the aspect of Divinity that enabled them to reach high levels of realization, and many of these were later modified into magnificent temples.

As the years rolled by, however, the monuments and temples began to attract archeologists and visitors, who knew little or nothing about the history of the adepts and the nature of the practices they had undertaken. Pilgrims regard such a site with reverence, but they usually focus their attention on the monument itself or on a temple that houses an altar or a statue, unaware that the actual shrine is not one particular spot, but the entire locale—a stretch of riverbank, a hilltop, an entire mountain valley, or a sizable tract of forest. Unfamiliar with the dynamics of the energy that vibrates throughout the area at a subtle level, they pay homage to the deity in a temple. The tantrics who still live in the vicinity continue to bask in that energy today as they conduct their prolonged practices in privacy.

Some shrines have been occupied for thousands of years by tantrics who have undertaken the same or a similar practice, and there the energy is so well-polarized that if we live in the vicinity and undertake a compatible practice we are naturally immersed in that stream of energy and glide toward the goal almost without effort. On the other hand, if we undertake a practice that is not compatible with the energy of the site we will confront formidable obstacles.

Other sites, such as Allahabad, have been the hub of hundreds of tantric practices, and therefore within the radius of a dozen miles or so almost any kind of tantric sadhana will be fruitful. And because thousands of devout practitioners and millions of faithful pilgrims visit Allahabad every year, they perpetuate the concentration of spiritual energy there. As a result this city is called *tirtha raja* (the lord of all shrines).

Just as we must go into a laboratory to gain a direct experience of the applied sciences and conduct repeated experiments to discover the strengths and weaknesses of our findings, so must we undertake practices at these shrines to gain an in-depth knowledge of tantra. If we visit a variety of them we will find that each has its own unique characteristics, and practicing there will bring its own specific revelation. The resulting experiences help us understand why some practices include certain disciplines and others do not, and why a particular shrine is conducive to a particular type of practice and disruptive to others.

Inexperienced students believe that the different schools of tantra are antithetical. They mistake a particular technique for the sum of tantra and have no way of resolving apparent contradictions among different disciplines. But after coming into contact with a variety of teachers and disciplines they will come to see that apparently contradictory tantric prac-tices are appropriate in a specific context and inappropriate in others, and that specific practices are meaningful at different levels of sadhana.

The experiences gained at these sites also teaches us to understand apparent discrepancies in the scriptures. Tantric

practices are rarely documented in a systematic or comprehensive manner. And until we understand the context in
which references to particular practices are made we will find
contradictions among different tantric texts. In some practices, for example, the use of meat and liquor is compulsory; in
others it is prohibited. Some scriptures prescribe sacrificing
the inner beast (the ego) by means of contemplation and
self-surrender; others prescribe sacrificing an animal to
achieve this same result.

Those with only a superficial knowledge of tantra will also
find a contradiction between the "left-hand" and "right-hand"
paths. Because left-hand tantrics do not hold conventional
standards of ethics and morality in high regard there is the
general impression that in addition to consuming meat and
fish in their practices, left-hand tantrics invariably drink
liquor and have sex as part of their rituals. On the other hand,
it is believed that right-hand tantrics are pure people who
maintain high standards of ethics and morality and condemn
the philosophy and practices of left-hand tantrics. They are
more "spiritual," it is thought, than those of the left-hand
path. This sense that there is a sharp dichotomy between the
two paths was not prevalent before writing books became a
profession; it has been created and perpetuated by those who
have neither studied the scriptures thoroughly nor visited
tantric shrines to observe how aspirants from both paths study
and practice under the guidance of the masters.

THE SHRINES AS TEACHERS

The apparent contradiction between the left- and right-
hand paths of tantra can be resolved by visiting the Kamakhya
shrine in Assam and doing practices there. This is a shrine
where animal sacrifice is still practiced—but the atmosphere
is permeated by an overwhelming air of compassion and

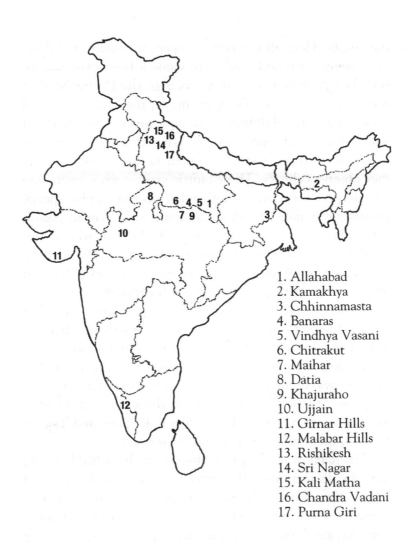

1. Allahabad
2. Kamakhya
3. Chhinnamasta
4. Banaras
5. Vindhya Vasani
6. Chitrakut
7. Maihar
8. Datia
9. Khajuraho
10. Ujjain
11. Girnar Hills
12. Malabar Hills
13. Rishikesh
14. Sri Nagar
15. Kali Matha
16. Chandra Vadani
17. Purna Giri

Location of tantric shrines

tranquility. Here all the pairs of opposites—light and darkness, compassion and cruelty, to name a few—exist side by
side. The protector of all living beings, the Divine Mother
Kamakhya, consumes flesh; Bhairava, the giver of mental
clarity and spiritual illumination, is pleased by the offering of
liquor. Tantrics at Kamakhya talk as if they invariably include
sex as the fifth and last step in their sadhana, but in reality
they observe celibacy. Those tantric masters who simply sing
the glory of the Divine Mother but do not display special
powers are honored by those aspirants who seem to possess
extraordinary tantric *siddhis* (powers). Anyone who is not
familiar with the basic metaphysics of tantra will find the
experience at this shrine disorienting. On the other hand, if
they come properly prepared they will experience the dance
of the destructive and creative aspects of divinity. In other
words, if you do not know how to see motherly affection
in both aspects of the divine force, the initial experience of
compassion and tranquility is soon replaced by fear, and you
will vow never to return. But if you are interested in unveiling
the mystery of left-hand tantra and the sublime method of
meditation on tantric goddesses like Kali, Tara, and Tripura
Sundari, then this is the right place for you.

The habit of allowing your attention to be pulled here and
there by distractions is the greatest obstacle to an extended
stay at Kamakhya. The next obstacle is an attraction to
miracles. The tantrics who deliberately perform miracles,
however, are shielding the true adepts from aspirants who are
merely seeking power and pleasure. If you are not distracted
by miracles you will meet a master. Incidentally, this is one of
the rare sites where you can find tantric adepts of all ten of the
esoteric paths known as the *maha vidyas*.

Another shrine, Chhinnamasta, in the jungles of Ram
Garh in the state of Bihar, is the locus for tantric sadhana

inspired by the goddess Chhinnamasta, a manifestation of the Divine Mother. The shrine itself consists of a tiny temple in the middle of nowhere, but the area within a radius of several miles is known for miraculous occurrences. Chhinnamasta represents the energy of transcendental consciousness, and in her personified form she is represented as a decapitated woman who holds a sword in her right hand and her own head in the left. On her left and right two other goddesses are drinking the blood that spouts from her neck. Like Jesus Christ she has given her body (to be taken as food) and her blood (as drink) to those she loves. If you know where to look you will find tantric adepts of this school; figuratively speaking they have beheaded themselves in order to find an eternal place at Chhinnamasta's feet.

If you want to cultivate the power and wisdom that will enable you to conquer your ego and offer the best of yourself to your fellow beings then you must visit this place. But, as scriptures like *Shakti Sangama Tantra* state, you must be ready to be beheaded symbolically (and perhaps even literally), for you gain immortality only after you are resurrected. Here you will certainly find someone who can explain the spiritual meaning of crucifixion and its role in attaining everlasting life. And the yogic techniques of leaving the body without dying and entering another body without being born (*parakaya pravesha*) are a specialty of the adepts belonging to the Chhinnamasta school of tantra.

Banaras in North India is another hub of tantric mystery, but walking through the streets of this ancient city you find what you seek only if you know how to search. All known or unknown spiritual traditions that ever existed in India have their roots here, but to a casual tourist the city is chaotic, noisy, and polluted; its streets are full of cows and lined with crowded temples. Without proper guidance and a well-defined goal you could roam endlessly without finding anything.

Banaras is an excellent destination for those who know nothing about tantra and are genuinely interested in learning; it is also an excellent destination for those who are intellectu- ally well-versed in tantric principles and are keen on gaining direct experience. But it is not the best place for those in between. Beginners can begin by studying with any known teacher, and soon they will understand how and where to find someone who can help them undertake an appropriate tantric practice. Those who are familiar with tantric principles and have begun practicing find that the spiritual energy emanat- ing from any of the shrines may become a living guide. Such aspirants do not waste their time trying to find a tantric master; instead, the divine force comes to them in some form (human or non-human), and such a blessed aspirant knows whether such experiences are genuine or illusory. Problems await the intermediate group: those who have read a little but have not done any practice. Such tantric enthusiasts are gullible and usually get lost in this spiritual mall.

This is another reason why knowledge of the scriptures is crucial. To those who have studied acclaimed tantric texts (such as *Netra Tantra*, *Swacchanda Tantra*, *Tantraloka*, *Rudra Yamala*, *Prapancha Sara*, and *Sri Vidyarnava*) Banaras is a tantric paradise. They will know exactly which path is perfect for them. They can, for example, walk directly to the shrine of Ganesha (known as Duddhiraja), receive his blessings, and then proceed to Kala Bhairava and with his permission enter the city of light (which, spiritually speaking, is situated at the tip of Shiva's trident—a city beyond the realm of earth). With clarity and confidence they can then walk into the temple complex of Kamaccha and by following the left-hand path of

Banaras

tantra gain experience within a few months which might take many years for them to gain elsewhere.

A little distance from Kamaccha lies the famous tantric shrine Krim Kunda, belonging to the *aughar* tradition. Here the fire lit by Baba Kinaram several hundred years ago is the living teacher, and under its guidance you may undertake the practice outlined in *Swacchanda Tantra*. The result, as promised by the living force of this site, is that you will attain the privilege of being guided by Bhairava, the most vibrant form of Shiva and the foremost master of tantric science. Ordinarily adepts belonging to this tradition are experts in the solar science (*surya vijñana*).

Once you have gained access to the inner circle of tantrics in any of these places you will discover that the spirit of their city awakens at night. This is when the tantric adepts begin their sadhana at these and other sites, including Durga Kund, Sankat Mochan, Varahi Temple, the area around Vishnath Temple, Annapurna, Lalita Ghat, Dashashwamedh Ghat, and Manikarnika, the most famous burning ghat.

Two hours south of Banaras in the foothills of the Vindhya mountains on a bank of the Ganga lies another tantric shrine, Vindhya Vasani, the abode of the combined forces of Lakshmi, Sarasvati, and Kali. The temples of these three goddesses form the three corners of a triangle, and the area encompassed by this triangle is like a yantra. Each temple is associated with a unique form of tantra sadhana. At the corner known as Kalikhoh, Kali is worshiped in a left-hand fashion; Sarasvati is worshiped in a right-hand fashion in the spot known as Astabhuja; and Lakshmi is worshiped in a way that combines both paths at the temple known as Vindhya Vasani. Tantric aspirants seeking results of a magical nature seek Kali at Kalikhoh; those seeking knowledge, retentive power (memory), a sharpened intellect, and success in the fine arts resort to Sarasvati at Astabhuja; while those seeking wealth undertake Lakshmi-related practices at Vindhya Vasani.

The area adjoining Astabhuja on the banks of the Ganga is where you will find the practitioners of "forbidden" tantra. But if you travel into the mountains toward Gerua Talub and Moltia Talab you will encounter tantrics of such a mysterious nature that they cannot be put in any category. (As you recall, this is where we met Bhuta Baba.) A group of scriptures known as the Puranas describe the spiritual significance of this area and explain why shakti sadhana undertaken at these sites bears remarkable fruit. Although the mountains in this vicinity are rocky and almost barren, the indescribable fragrance of the air transports you to a dimension never before experienced. And you can clearly feel the presence of the living masters as you approach the little monuments built in honor of the adepts who have here taken *bhumi samadhi* (the practice of voluntarily casting off the body underground) with the determination to undertake a prolonged meditation. If you have read genuine tantric texts and visit this place you feel compelled to know more about these masters and the advanced tantric practices they have undertaken there.

If you move further south in the Vindhya range you will come upon Chitrakut, where the ashram of Sage Atri and Mother Anasuya, situated on a bank of the Mandakini River, is as vibrant today as it was thousands of years ago. Among the group of sadhus, called *vairagi*, who dominate this locale you will find tantric adepts practicing the disciplines associated with the tradition of Dattatreya, the master of masters. The nature of their sadhana is such that through the millennia this mountain has become an embodiment of love, compassion, kindness, and complete surrender. In fact through their practice these adepts have so charged a hill in the Chitrakut region that it is known as Kamada Giri, the wish-yielding mountain. You can clearly sense divinity manifesting through every aspect of nature, granting the grace and guidance necessary for a successful sadhana. But if a practice undertaken here is not in conformity with these characteristics, the practitioner will feel uncomfortable. Up to the late 1950s, before a well-known saint named Bhole Prabhu moved the manuscripts to Allahabad, the monasteries in this region were significant repositories of tantric scriptures.

Still further south in the Vindhya mountains lies a shakti shrine known as Maihar, where the flavor of tantric practices is totally different from those you find in Chitrakut. This is a site of miracles. Faithful pilgrims flock here to receive the healing grace of the goddess Matangi, known locally as Maihar Ki Devi, and tantrics intent on cultivating healing power and creativity in the arts find this shrine most suitable to their practice. People believe that Alha, a great warrior and the permanent attendant of the goddess, became immortal through her grace, and visits this shrine every night. Every now and then seekers in this area report that they have received guidance from him.

Although it is not well-known, one of the most mystical tantric shrines lies in Datia, a small town near Jhansi in central India. This site is associated with Bagalamukhi, one of the ten great goddesses. The queen of forbidden tantra, she embodies the power of immobilization. Her tantric name, Brahmastra (literally "the supreme weapon"), is an indication of the unimaginable power contained in this particular sadhana. There is no higher tantric practice for cutting asunder the snares of ignorance and taming the inner beast (the ego). However, undertaking this sadhana is so demanding that it is like setting out to reclaim a precious gem from the jaws of a shark. The most illustrious adept of this path, Datia Wale

Swami, left his body in 1979, but the intense practices related to this path still continue.

Khajuraho, another tantric site in central India, is dramatically different from all the places mentioned so far—it consists of more than a dozen temples, whose walls are covered with erotic statues of yogis and yoginis performing various tantric mudras. Due to its sensual appeal Khajuraho has been overrun by tourists from India and abroad, so you may not encounter tantrics at this site today. But if you have a basic background in tantrism you will find that the walls picture tantric practices that incorporate the use of liquor and sex. A tour through Khajuraho will leave you either with the impression that tantrism is a path of sexual insanity or with the understanding that it is a way of transforming this natural urge into a spiritual means.

Like Banaras, the city of Ujjain in central India is a hub of many tantric traditions and the practices associated with them. Mahakala, the devourer of time, or the destroyer of death, presides over all other deities residing here, but practices from many traditions are often found in the same ritual. The central focus of the early morning worship of Mahakala, for example, involves smearing the shiva lingam with ash from the cremation ground, as well as elements from astrology, alchemy, rituals, and purely meditative yogic techniques. Nowhere else will you find such a perfect blend of so many disparate elements.

For ages Ujjain was the center of astronomical research, where tantric *sadhakas* studied the nature and movement of the stars and planets and discovered the connecting links between the celestial realm and the human body. Those who are familiar with tantric astrology will have no trouble understanding why a certain practice associated with the shrine of Mangalanatha (Mars) in Ujjain can affect our worldly prosperity by influencing the forces in our body and mind that correspond to Mars.

The walls and ceiling of the Hara Siddha Gauri temple in Ujjain are like a living library. Here you will find an elaborate Sri Chakra with hundreds of deities depicted in their personified form. To a student of tantra familiar with the basic scriptures of Sri Chakra an hour-long visit to this temple is equivalent to several years of study in a conventional library.

A visit to the Kala Bhairava temple nearby will change your belief system if you happen to witness the statue of Kala Bhairava apparently drinking liquor—a phenomenon that occurs frequently. The liquor actually disappears from the chalice. After seeing this your curiosity regarding left-hand tantra will turn into a burning desire to practice and unveil the mystery for yourself.

Five hundred yards from this temple, at the cremation ground on the riverbank, is the shrine of Vikranta Bhairava, a place famous for the quick acquisition of startling *siddhis*, or supernatural powers. Here, in the dead of night, tantrics who are lovers of the destructive force celebrate the eternal sport of the creator. And if you are persistent you will meet tantric adepts like Dabral Baba, a spiritual figure noted for his clairvoyance.

Far to the west in the hills of Girnar in the state of Gujarat the tantric masters are hidden in monasteries or living in ashrams. By and large they belong to the tradition of Dattatreya and Gorakhnatha, and they are unique in their ability to combine alchemy with tantric practices.

On the other hand, the tantrics living in the hills of Malabar in South India are characterized by their knowledge of shakti sadhana, especially Sri Vidya. The majority of them are householders who adhere strictly to the puritan values of orthodox brahmins, and in their system of tantra sadhana the use of liquor, meat, and other "morally impure" components is not permitted. Here right-hand tantra is practiced in its purest form.

And finally, if you go to the Himalayan region in North India you will find the full spectrum of tantra. Every village has a shrine, a guardian deity, and a set of practices to propitiate this deity, who, according to their faith, gives them protection and nourishment. Whether they know it or not, the way in which these villagers connect their hearts with the deity is purely tantric. Uneducated, they lack access to the scriptures, but they follow family traditions which have been passed down for untold generations. To them the deity residing in the local shrine is a part of their family, and they grow up with the belief that they themselves are an integral part of nature's family, like the plants, animals, rivers, and mountains.

This is the fundamental philosophy of tantra, and the practices of the Himalayan villagers are molded by it. They are pure and innocent—nature has taught them honesty and simplicity. Content with life, they continue their spiritual pursuits in the manner they have learned from their elders and teachers. They believe that the deity at the local shrine is part of them and they are part of Her; they come from Her, live under Her protection, and after death they go back to Her. The villagers who know the scriptures consider the same deity to be the manifestation of the highest truth. And by following more systematic and comprehensive tantric practices than those done by the uneducated villagers, they attempt to experience universal consciousness by merging with Her.

These different levels of understanding both the Divinity and the purpose of life have led to different approaches for gaining Her grace and guidance. This is how the tantric practices have become so diverse. For example, one person worships the deity so that his goats will be healthy and fertile, another so that her children will marry into a suitable family, while others worship and meditate on Her in order to attain freedom from the cycle of births and deaths. To express their love and devotion to the Divinity some offer vegetarian food, while others sacrifice a goat. Still others surrender their ego to the Divine. Some connect their hearts with the Divine by means of simple tantric practices like offering incense, flowers, water, and fruit to the fire, along with the recitation of prayers and mantras. Others, who are familiar with the symbolic meaning of yantras, have developed more elaborate rituals. They know that different components of the yantras represent the invisible forces of individual and collective consciousness, so they incorporate the visualization and worship of yantra into their practices. And in the same village there may be someone endowed with the understanding that the human body is a miniature universe—a perfect yantra for meditating on the highest reality. Such a one has a purely meditative approach to tantra and aims to experience oneness with the primordial Divinity without any ritual involvement at all.

Not only does the method of worship vary from villager to villager, the practices themselves can change. For example approximately one hundred kilometers northeast of Rishikesh there is a town called Sri Nagar ("Sri Nagar" means "Sri Vidya, city of the tantric goddess"), because long ago hundreds of tantric adepts and aspirants, especially those belonging to the tradition of Sri Vidya, did their practices there. The most significant shrine in this area is not a temple or statue of the goddess, but a huge boulder lying in the riverbed on the outskirts of town. It is regarded as a living Sri Yantra (also known as Sri Chakra), the most complex of all yantras. Here in this yantra, tantrics propitiated the Divine Mother in the form of Sri Vidya.

The inverted boulder at Sri Nagar

Twelve hundred years ago when the great master Shankaracharya visited Sri Nagar he learned that this yantra was worshipped with a daily animal sacrifice (human sacrifices were also offered on occasion), a practice of left-hand tantra. As the legend goes, Shankaracharya, after performing an elaborate ritual worship, turned the boulder upside down, hiding the yantra from view. And since that time the Sri Chakra has not been worshipped in a left-hand fashion at Sri Nagar.

Shankaracharya was an influential master and a proponent of only those aspects of tantric wisdom that did not contradict the social, moral, and ethical values upheld in the Vedic scriptures. Wherever he went he lifted human consciousness by teaching that there is only one reality, which manifests in all names and forms, and that there is a definite way to gain the experience of the oneness that runs throughout diversity. As this experience matures we spontaneously come to love all and exclude none, and the higher virtues of non-violence, love, compassion, and kindness manifest from the experience of unitary consciousness. Rituals can serve as a stepping-stone to gain this experience, he taught, and if rituals abide with the principle of non-violence, the Divinity within and without is pleased.

By introducing this concept in Sri Nagar and other places Shankaracharya influenced the prevailing belief system, and this in turn brought modifications in spiritual practices. But by no means did he completely wipe out the system of left-hand practices. Today in Sri Nagar and its surrounding area as well as nearby Kali Matha and Chandra Vadani there are tantric practitioners who still follow both the left- and right-hand paths.

Another shrine, Purna Giri in the Almora district of the Himalayas, is famous for tantric practices of the *samaya* school. These tantrics do not employ any external means to awaken the primordial Shakti within; their method is purely meditative. The mountaintop itself is the shrine, and pilgrims who need a focus for their devotion pay homage to an ancient tree growing on the mountaintop. Purna Giri is one of the main pilgrimage sites for tantric adepts of the Shankaracharya order, and the practices undertaken here do not involve rituals. The goal of the practices, as described in the scriptures, is pure spiritual illumination without the slightest trace of worldliness. In fact the literal meaning of "Purna Giri" is "the mountain leading to perfection" or "the mountain that embodies perfect fulfillment."

According to the scriptures this shrine corresponds to the *sahasrara* chakra, or crown center, one of the principal centers of consciousness within the body. Just as the brain witnesses the actions it initiates without being involved in them, so must aspirants who undertake practices at this shrine help others without becoming involved with them. In order to see and understand itself the brain does not need help from outside; similarly, in order to gain a direct experience of the reality that resides at the crown center there is no need for external rituals at the Purna Giri shrine.

In contrast, rituals are a necessary component of the practices undertaken at the Kamakhya shrine in Assam, for that shrine is associated with the first and second chakras. Witnessing alone does not help in resolving and satisfying the issues related to the first and second chakras: hunger, fear, desire, and the urge for sense gratification. Those urges have to be dealt with more directly, in a manner that actually involves the senses, so transforming them into a spiritual means is the inner purpose of the rituals performed at Kamakhya. If this has not yet been accomplished there is no point in doing sadhana at Purna Giri.

All of the shrines discussed in this chapter are centers of tantric practice and discipline. Their role is central. Studying at a recognized university ensures the quality of your education, and the knowledge gained there is expected to be definitive and reliable. That is also true of tantric studies. If you wish to acquire authentic knowledge, grounded in direct experience, you cannot overlook these shrines.

Asking why these shrines are found only in India is like asking why Oxford is in England and Harvard is in Massachusetts. The site is appropriate to the practice. Academic institutions require buildings, labs, and libraries, but in the case of tantric institutions none of this external paraphernalia is required. The energy of these shrines is not confined to a particular physical structure, either natural or man-made. Rather, the space in the vicinity of a shrine is itself so charged with energy that it serves as an ever-present and fully furnished library and laboratory. Tantric practitioners who know how to tap into this energy can connect it with the corresponding energy within their own body and mind. And because space is indestructible, it makes no difference if temples and monasteries are constructed or destroyed. Nor does it make any difference if the physical characteristics of the site are completely altered. One of the names for Banaras, which is now one of the most congested cities in India, is still *Ananda Vana* (the forest of bliss). The collective consciousness of this holy place does not register bricks and mortar, noise and pollution: from time to time the city is built and destroyed; temples are replaced by mosques, which are replaced by temples; religious tensions and political unrest affect the minds of the residents—but such happenings have no effect on or in the space which is filled with divine consciousness. Seekers and adepts associate with that eternal Banaras—Kashi, the City of Light.

Chapter Three

FINDING THE WAY IN

antrics hold that there is only one primordial force animating all forms of life, that this force is the Divine, and that the world is Her manifestation. For them experiencing this divinity in every aspect of life is liberation, and anything less is bondage. That is why to them worldly success is not an obstacle to spiritual growth; on the contrary it is the ground for spiritual success, because those who are without worldly means and resources have little time and energy for spiritual endeavors. Most of our problems, tantrics maintain, are not caused because we do not know God; rather, we suffer because we do not know this world. But once we know what this material world is all about and can regulate the subtle forces that govern it, we can overcome all suffering.

THE SPECTRUM OF PRACTICES

Because tantrics do not accept the notion that spirituality and worldliness cannot commingle, tantra addresses all the concerns of both body and spirit. It is up to us, the tantrics say, to choose the nature and scope of the practices we undertake. Highly evolved practices, such as those pertaining to the tradition of Sri Vidya, address all aspects of life, while practices with narrower objectives may address just one or two of life's concerns.

These concerns run the gamut of human experience, from the base to the lofty. In the vast tantric literature there are practices that can be regarded as a form of black magic. For example *Dattatreya Tantra* describes a practice for driving an enemy insane. It involves concentrating the negative forces of the mind on feathers from two natural enemies (an owl and a crow), and further charging these feathers with rituals consisting of ingredients which reinforce the animosity, such as the fruit of the nux plant, red chilies, salt, and the paste and smoke created by bitter objects such as neem (*Azadirachta indicia*). The practice is done on the night of the new moon and is concluded by burying the feathers along with the other ritual ingredients in mud, preferably under a neem tree. The entire procedure is accompanied by the recitation of a specific mantra.

If we have not seen the effect of such practices through our own eyes we can dismiss them as superstition. But once we understand that plants, minerals, animals, and humans are all the locus for nature's subtle forces we can find a scientific explanation for why these practices work. Homeopathic medicines, which are diluted to the point at which no physical trace remains of the original substance, work at the level of energy. In the same way the feathers of an owl and a crow contain the subtle impression of animosity. And once this animosity is awakened with the use of rituals and the energy polarized in a certain direction with the power of sound (mantra) and mind, it can affect a person with a weak will.

At the other end of the spectrum there are practices that expedite our meditation and bring us closer to the inner light.

Unlike negative practices such as the one just described, these positive practices incorporate spiritually illuminating and rejuvenating ingredients, such as lotus, ghee, brahmi (Bacopa monniera), sesame seeds, and guggul (Commiphora mukul). Like the negative tantric practices, these positive practices greatly intensify whatever is undertaken. For example according to the scriptures the gayatri mantra helps us wash off karmic impurities, and it is therefore one of the most powerful mantras for purifying the mind and heart. As this process begins we gain clarity of mind, our thoughts become organized, and our concentration improves, enabling us to intuitively distinguish good from bad and right from wrong. Ordinarily, however, when people meditate on the gayatri mantra it takes years before they notice any effect. The tantric method of practicing gayatri accelerates this process. It includes rituals, meditation on a specific yantra, meditation on the chakras, the recitation of auxiliary mantras, pranayama practices, and, ultimately, the making of a fire offering.

In tantra the gayatri mantra can be used in several ways to achieve worldly goals, to overcome specific obstacles, or to advance spiritually. Offering a mixture of sugar, honey, coconut, ghee, and kaner (Nerium indicum) into the fire while repeating the gayatri mantra cures physical and psychosomatic problems. Offering the flower of a lotus while reciting the gayatri mantra brings prosperity. Offering the fruit, leaves, and sticks from a bilva tree (Aegle marmelos) brings both peace and prosperity. Offering karanja fruit (Pongamia pinnata) is a tantric cure for phobia and schizophrenia. An offering of sticks from a palash tree (Butea monosperma) grants retentive power (memory) and clarity of mind.

Similarly, chapter 6 of Netra Tantra describes six ways to use the maha mrityunjaya mantra for healing oneself or others. Most of these consist of rituals, visualization, and meditation on different chakras. Other scriptures, such as *Swacchanda Tantra* and *Sri Vidyarnava*, describe practices that can be undertaken at the cremation ground, or in a banyan tree, or under it. They are usually accompanied by meditation on the corresponding yantra, during which a wide variety of materials—ranging from incense, flowers, water, herbs, and fruits, to cooked food, meat, and liquor—are offered to the divinity invoked in the yantra.

The goal of the practice determines what ritual ingredients are used. They can include water, flowers, milk, yogurt, ghee (clarified butter), fruit, cooked food, honey, turmeric, rice, black sesame seeds, raw sugar, sandalwood powder, saffron, and, in some cases, liquor, meat, and fish. And because it is necessary for the practitioner to maintain a mood that is compatible with the force being invoked, the goal of the practice also dictates what that mood should be—tense, relaxed, passive, aggressive, etc.

To engender the most auspicious atmosphere, the practitioner eats food that is compatible with the practice, selects a compatible set of mala beads, wears clothes of a compatible color, and chooses a compatible material on which to sit while doing the practice. For example if the goal of your practice is to subdue an enemy, to destroy the animosity in an enemy's mind, or to subdue the enemies within yourself (the negative tendencies of the mind, such as ego, attachment, desire, and anger), your diet preceding the practice should consist of yellow food—dishes containing turmeric, saffron, or yellow legumes (such as toor dahl and mung dahl). Rice pudding with saffron or a pudding of cream of wheat, puffed lotus seeds, and saffron is ideal. A mala made of rudraksha beads, turmeric root, coral, or topaz will be conducive to engendering the proper mood, as will wearing yellow clothes (preferably silk) and sitting on a woolen blanket.

In all the practices described so far rituals play the key role, but tantric texts also describe practices that do not involve rituals and therefore do not employ external objects. These practices are purely meditative; rituals are replaced by internal, contemplative techniques.

For example because tantrics consider the human body to be a microcosm of the entire universe, tantrics who use meditative practices instead of rituals invoke the forces of nature within their own body instead of those same forces in external objects. The goal is the same: experiencing a state of oneness with those forces. Their ritual consists mainly of reciting mantras while concentrating on certain parts of their body. They do not use external yantras: their body is the yantra. Nor do they use fire rituals to propitiate the life-force: their own solar plexus serves as the fire bowl. With their powers of concentration they visualize the mind as a garden where all kinds of desires grow in the form of flowers—they can gather a flower of any color and fragrance for any particular practice. They offer their own ego into the fire at the solar plexus in place of clarified butter.

The scriptures that describe this kind of practice make a comprehensive and minutely detailed equation between the forces of the cosmos and the forces in the body. For example they pinpoint nine minerals, nine gems, and nine groups of herbs that correspond to the nine planets; ultimately these groups of nine correspond to the nine constituents of the human body: chyme, blood, flesh, fat, bone, marrow, seminal fluid, *ojas*, and *jiva*.

There is a third category of tantric practice that combines both ritual and meditation. Some tantrics may undertake the practice of the gayatri mantra, for example, in a purely ritualistic fashion. Then after completing a course of practice (which may consist of repeating the mantra a hundred thousand times, or eleven hundred thousand times, or 2.4 million times), they do a fire offering with sesame seeds and ghee while they continue to repeat the gayatri mantra. Then they go on to the next stage of the practice, which involves doing half of the daily gayatri practice while employing external ritualistic objects and the other half while meditating on the third chakra (the navel center). At this stage surrendering the ego to the fire element at the navel center replaces the offering of sesame seeds and ghee into the external ritual fire. At the third stage of practice they do not incorporate external rituals at all—the practice has become completely internal.

THE THREE SCHOOLS OF TANTRA

Over time the tantrics developed so many techniques that it became impossible to study them systematically or even to find a progression from one type of practice to another. So the adepts made an attempt to categorize them, using as a guide the journey from gross to subtle, from the external to the internal realm. And on the basis of this simple reasoning they divided all tantric practices and techniques into three major categories: those employing external objects, those which are purely meditative, and those which combine both techniques. This is the basis for the three major schools of tantra.

Most humans operate at the level of body consciousness: our sense of pleasure and pain and our experience of success and failure correspond to our bodies and to the world around us. So all the tantric practices requiring the involvement of our bodies, senses, and material objects were organized into one group called *kaula*—literally, "that which is related to *kula* (the family)." This is the path of householders. Practices accompanied by rituals, the recitation of scripture, pilgrimage to holy shrines, and fire offerings belong to the kaula path. The goal of tantric practices at this level is to organize life in

THE THREE SCHOOLS OF TANTRA

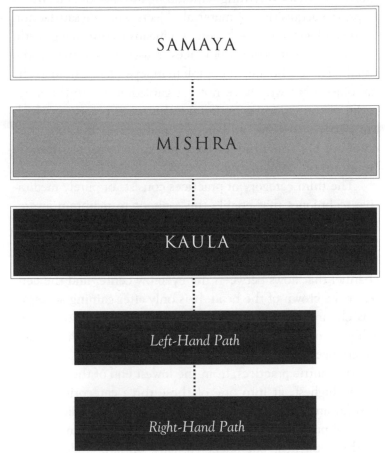

SAMAYA

MISHRA

KAULA

Left-Hand Path

Right-Hand Path

such a way that everything—including interpersonal relation-ships, the acquisition of material objects, and the satisfaction of the biological urges—becomes a means to spiritual growth.

Another category of practices is used to internalize the rituals. Those who aim at complete independence from exter-nal objects but who have not yet gained access to the inner realm of consciousness undertake this set of practices, which are partly ritualistic and partly meditative. Because they combine both techniques they are called *mishra*, literally "mixture" or "combination."

The third category of practices consists of purely medita-tive techniques that enable the aspirant to maintain aware-ness of their oneness with the Divine within. This school of tantra is called *samaya*, which means "one with Her." Its goal is to allow consciousness to move upward through the energy channel that flows between the eyebrow center and the cen-ter at the crown of the head. It is only after gaining access to this channel, called the *brahma nadi*, that practitioners can achieve their goal of meditating at the crown chakra and experience their oneness with the Divine Mother.

All tantric practices, from the lowest end of the spectrum to the highest, fit into one of these three categories: kaula, mishra, and samaya; they refer to external, combined, and internal practices. There is no strict rule holding an aspirant to this sequence, but adepts usually initiate students into kaula practices first. Even before this, however, students are led through a preliminary series of practices, beginning with standard mantra meditation and followed by the tantric way of meditating on that mantra. Only then is the corresponding yantra introduced, along with the practice of rituals.

Unfortunately the majority of students stop their quest at this point and start to experiment with tantric techniques that aim at cultivating the power to perform miracles. According

DISTINCTIVE FEATURES OF THE THREE SCHOOLS

Kaula	Mishra	Samaya
Those following the path of kaula	Those following the path of mishra	Those following the path of samaya
Perform external rituals	Perform both external rituals and mental worship	Practice only internal meditation
Worship the Divine Mother in the muladhara chakra	Worship the Divine Mother in the heart center	Meditate only in the sahasrara
Worship kundalini in the muladhara while she is still asleep	Worship kundalini in the heart center in the form of Ishta Deva, while visualizing her as fully awake	Begin meditation only after kundalini is awakened
Use objects in their ritual worship	Use objects as well as their mental substitutes in their ritual worship	Use no objects and no ritual worship
Use liquor, meat, fish, mudras, and physical union in their rituals	Do not use liquor, meat, fish, mudras, and physical union in their rituals	Never use liquor, meat, fish, mudras, and physical union in any practice
Draw, carve, or inscribe the yantra on a physical object	Draw the yantra on their palm or simply visualize it in the heart center	View the body as a yantra
Draw and worship a yantra according to samhara krama, the method of withdrawal	Draw and worship the yantra according to sthiti krama, the method of maintenance	Worship the yantra of the human body according to srishti krama, the method of creation
Aim to attain both bhoga (worldly enjoyment) and moksha (spiritual freedom)	Aim to attain both bhoga and moksha, with emphasis on moksha	Aim only to attain moksha, spiritual freedom

to the scriptures, however, to concentrate on such powers is a distraction and an obstacle to spiritual growth; if we are not diligent, some of them can be injurious. That is why such practices are called "forbidden tantra." But if we do not become entangled at this level of achievement, further initiations lead us to discover the mishra and samaya level of tantric mysteries. The first step is to become familiar with the kaula theory and practice, including the distinction between the right- and left-hand paths within the path of kaula.

KAULA TANTRA

As already mentioned, the word *kaula* is derived from *kula*, which means "family"; those tantrics who believe that every aspect of creation is part of a divine family are called "kaulas." They believe that Shakti, the Divine Mother, is the origin of all that exists. Everything—all forms of matter and energy—emerge from Her. It is not that the universe as a distinct entity evolves from Her; rather, She *becomes* the universe, She *is* the universe. She is both inside the universe and beyond it. Considering anything to be different from Her is ignorance, and experiencing anything as other than Her is bondage. Liberation is experiencing Her alone, within and without. Becoming one with Her in every respect is the highest achievement.

Kaula tantrics practice this philosophy in every aspect of their daily lives. First they cultivate a positive attitude toward their relationships with their family, environment, society, and, ultimately, the entire world. The process of self-transformation they undertake is guided by this philosophy—they see their spouse, children, friends, and even enemies as the manifestation of the Divine Mother. And because they have dismantled the wall that ordinarily stands between right and wrong, good and evil, auspicious and inauspicious, they do not find worldly objects and experiences to be a barrier in their spiritual quest. They see the Divine Mother in everything, so they see no need to renounce the world in order to find Her.

Tantrics commit themselves to sadhana in order to bring this philosophy into the realm of direct experience. To accomplish this the first and most important step is to analyze our own consciousness to find out how effortlessly we are able to live with the philosophy. On the practical level few of us experience our oneness with the Divine Mother, and even if we do the experience is momentary. Instead we experience a sense of separateness and a longing to be connected with Her. According to the adepts this is the root cause of all loneliness and fear, and it cannot be overcome until we are established in non-dualistic consciousness.

In most of us, however, the perception of duality is so strong that not only do we experience ourselves as totally different from the all-pervading Divine Force, we also feel that this separation is intrinsic to our existence. We identify with the physical realm so strongly that we experience our self-existence only in terms of our bodies. In other words, because we do not see ourselves as having any existence beyond the physical, our experience of pleasure and pain, loss and gain is totally body-centered. We find ourselves driven by the four primitive urges—food, sex, sleep, and self-preservation—from which spring emotions such as desire, anger, hatred, jealousy, and greed. And until we find a way to establish ourselves in non-dual unitary consciousness these negative emotions constantly flood our mind and nervous system with anxiety, fear, and a pervasive sense of insecurity. This is the level on which animals operate.

Unlike animals, however, our thoughts, feelings, and actions are not always motivated by the need for food, sex, sleep, and self-preservation, and our consciousness is not confined to our bodies. As our awareness becomes more refined we attain a degree of freedom from these urges, even though we are at their mercy to some extent as long as we identify with the body. There is no question, however, that staying alive requires maintaining some degree of body consciousness—the association of consciousness with the body is what keeps us here, and that is why kaula practitioners insist that there is no point in condemning the primitive urges. Instead we must learn the techniques for managing and using them wisely.

THE LEFT-HAND AND RIGHT-HAND PATHS OF KAULA

Kaula tantrics approach the four primitive urges in one of two ways. Followers of the right-hand path believe that the less active these urges are, the less distraction they will create. Their sadhana, therefore, is to practice self-restraint and subdue the basic urges until these urges have no power to distract them from their spiritual focus. Followers of the left-hand path maintain that these urges are intrinsic and that restraining them cripples our body, mind, and senses. They believe that it is better to follow the law of nature and let the biological urges express themselves in a healthy manner, but without indulging them. According to these tantrics the key is learning to channel these powerful drives in a spiritual direction.

The right-hand kaula tantrics have developed a complex system of rituals to create a bridge between themselves and the Divine. They follow the principles of asceticism. The observances that go along with their rituals (such as fasting or eating very little, observing silence, and refraining from thinking and speaking in a way that stimulates the desire for pleasure and bodily comforts) are designed to subdue the primitive urges through imposing a high degree

DISTINCTIVE FEATURES OF THE TWO KAULA SCHOOLS

Right-Hand Path (Dakshina Marga)	Left-Hand Path (Vama Marga)
Those who follow this path	Those who follow this path
Perform external rituals while using only "pure" objects	Make no distinction between pure and impure
Hold puritan views	Hold unorthodox views
Emphasize austerities	Emphasize moderation
Condemn the use of liquor, meat, fish, and physical union	Employ liquor, meat, fish, and physical union in select rituals
Strive to attain siddhis by propitiating the sattvic form of the Divinity	Strive to attain siddhis by all possible means
Encourage only practices that do not violate the principles of "purity" and conventional morality	Dare to undertake practices of any kind, including "forbidden" ones

of self-restraint. They draw a clear distinction between "pure" and "impure" ritual objects and observe this distinction in their daily lives. Their ascetic observances may make them physically weak for a time, but the observances are spiritually strengthening.

Left-hand kaula tantrics are not ascetics. On the contrary. Their rituals do not suppress the biological needs, because to consider anything impure or inauspicious, they feel, is to condemn the Divine Mother. And because She is the only reality, any sense of duality, including all aspects of body consciousness, is Her manifestation. The Divine Mother is the embodiment of supreme beauty, bliss, auspiciousness, and goodness, and so it follows that these characteristics are inherent in everything that exists. The body is Her manifestation, as are the senses, the primitive urges, and all of our thoughts and feelings. The perceptual world evolving from the Most Auspicious One cannot be inauspicious. According to the left-hand kaula tantrics, repressing the biological urges and imposing restraints that weaken the body and senses means that we are condemning them as well as the life-force that animates them. This is the hallmark not of spirituality but of ignorance. It is this group of left-hand kaula tantrics that employs liquor, meat, fish, mudras, and physical union in their rituals.

Scholars tell us that right- and left-hand tantra are mutually exclusive. They are not. In actual practice, initiation into left-hand disciplines constitutes the final stage of sadhana within the kaula school. Left-hand techniques are far more advanced than right-hand techniques, and only those who have first disciplined themselves by practicing right-hand kaula tantra are qualified to follow the left-hand path. In short, right- and left-hand disciplines do not constitute two distinct traditions; they are two different sets of discipline within the same school.

It is relatively easy to learn the practices of right-hand tantra and get initiated, but it is very difficult to find a master who will initiate you into the practices of left-hand tantra. The scriptures speak with one voice: "Kaula—especially the left-hand aspect—is an impenetrable mystery. The slightest carelessness on this path can lead to indulgence. It is easy for the mind to justify acts of sense gratification." I have observed that the adepts of this path rarely reveal themselves. They may practice left-hand tantra in private, but they generally teach only the techniques of the right-hand path. And before they do reveal themselves they lead their students through a series of arduous tests while they are still involved in the practices of right-hand tantra. The masters want to make sure the aspirant has no craving for sense gratification and will uphold the sacredness of this path.

To summarize: the complete knowledge and practice pertaining to the kaula school is traditionally imparted in three stages. Each consists of a specific kind of practice, and to get that practice directly from a master a student goes through a formal process of initiation. There are three levels of initiation. The first two help the aspirant unveil the mystery of the right-hand path of the kaula school. The third and final initiation allows the aspirant to gain access to left-hand kaula tantra. And it is only after going through these three levels of initiation and doing the practices that accompany them that we can systematically unveil the dynamics of matter and spirit, attain mastery over the forces governing life within and without, and take charge of our destiny.

Chapter Four

THE FIRST INITIATION: MANTRA

*W*e saw in chapter 3 that tantric practice begins with kaula tantra, and kaula tantra, in turn, begins with doing mantra japa in a right-hand (or purely meditative) manner. Then, after a student has practiced this standard form of mantra meditation for a while, he or she is initiated into the tantric method which includes many additional elements. In the tantric tradition the mantra is not simply an object for focusing the mind: the mantra is the illuminator of the mind. It is the body of the Divine Force in the form of sound. It is the living Divinity, and in the first level of practice the mind, body, and senses are employed to serve it. Constant repetition of mantra charges our being with divine consciousness, even-tually transforming our egocentric awareness into divine awareness. And when at the culmination of our sadhana we become one with the power of the mantra, the gap between individual and universal consciousness is filled. We are no longer a drop in the ocean; we become the ocean.

In the tantric tradition the anthropomorphic (personi-fied) form of the Divine is secondary to the mantric form. In fact the anthropomorphic form is merely a means of apprehending the mantric form. Tantric philosophy asserts that there is only one primordial life-force, known as Sri Vidya or Sri Mata (the Divine Mother). Just as the sun emits numberless rays, so do an infinite number of mantras emerge from the Divine Mother, and through systematic practice of these mantras Her imperceptible primordial force becomes so concentrated that a practitioner experiences it. When this happens it is called *darshana*—the direct vision of the invisible, absolute reality.

Tantrics do not place much value on anthropomorphic gods and goddesses. They tell versions of the following story to illustrate how ridiculous (and fruitless) it is to project human characteristics onto God.

There was once a brahmin priest who earned his livelihood by performing religious services for the people in his village. He was known for his devotion to the god Vishnu, and people regarded him as a holy man. Among his hundreds of followers was a shepherd who wanted to see God—even though he had no idea of what God was. His sheep did not require much attention, so he had plenty of time to visit the priest and barrage him with questions about God. "Why does Vishnu have four arms?" he would ask. "Why does he always sleep on a snake? Why does he have a lotus growing from his navel? Why does his wife just sit next to him without doing anything? If Vishnu is God, then who is Shiva? Which of them is the most powerful? Is there any God higher than Vishnu and Shiva? Which kind of God is the most powerful and kind to human beings?"

The priest gave the shepherd all kinds of philosophical answers, even explaining the symbolic meaning of the different limbs, weapons, and other characteristics of the gods, but the shepherd was so dense he could not grasp any of these theological answers. Finally, in frustration, the priest thought of how to explain God in a way that made sense to the simple man. He convinced the shepherd that

God looks like a sheep—the healthiest and most beautiful sheep ever known. He then instructed the shepherd to go into the forest and pray to this Sheep God and not to eat, drink, or sleep until He appeared. Delighted, the shepherd did exactly as the priest instructed.

On the third day, God came. But he looked like Vishnu, not like a sheep. "I am pleased with your devotion," Vishnu said. "Tell me, what boon do you wish from me?"

Startled, the shepherd asked, "Who are you? You are beautiful, but what are you doing here in the forest?"

"I am God," Vishnu replied. "You have been praying to me."

"God looks like a sheep," the shepherd retorted. "You are a fake. Don't waste my time."

So Vishnu left. An hour later the Sheep God came. He too said, "I am pleased with your devotion. Tell me, what boon do you wish from me?"

This time the shepherd was overwhelmed. He got up and greeted God, yet he wondered how a sheep could speak in human language and suspected that he was being tricked again. So he said, "You look like God, but why are you speaking in the human tongue?"

Immediately God emitted a magnificent bleat. Then he said, "That is how I usually speak, but unless I speak your language, how can you understand?"

The shepherd was still a bit skeptical, so he asked God to come with him so his priest could verify that he was really God.

"Wonderful," God replied. "Lead the way and I will follow."

"You might change your mind," the shepherd replied. "Let me take you by the ear."

So it was that the shepherd arrived at the home of the priest leading God by the ear. "Look, sir!" he called. "God is here!"

Annoyed, the priest came out and shouted at the shepherd. "It's a sheep, idiot! You have lost your mind."

The shepherd began praying, "O God, help my priest to under-stand you."

The priest was also praying: "O Lord, help this foolish man to understand you."

As they prayed, God appeared simultaneously as Vishnu to the priest and as a sheep to the shepherd. At least, that's how they perceived it.

When the priest fell at the feet of Vishnu the shepherd thought he was prostrating to the Sheep, so he too prostrated.

Both were happy because they had seen God. They were grateful to each other for a few hours—but by the next day they had resumed their old habits.

As this story shows, in order to bring the concept of Divinity closer to our daily experience we humans tend to superimpose mundane characteristics onto God, characteris-tics that are compatible with our personal preferences and beliefs. In most religions, for example, God seems to have little to do but reward those who worship Him and punish those who don't. In the Puranas there is a story about how the god Indra became furious when people stopped worshipping him, so he visited them with torrential rainstorms. In fact the anthropomorphic gods seem to have all the same problems humans do. Their egos collide; they get into wars; they become infatuated with others' wives (sometimes even resorting to rape); and they are punished by gods of a higher rank. Such gods, tantrics maintain, are simply figments of our imagination. Their behavior shows that they are not God.

The Sanskrit word for God is *Ishvara*, which means "the force capable of doing what She wishes to do, capable of not doing what He does not wish to do, and capable of undoing whatever so far has been done." God is the omniscient, omnipotent, and omnipresent primordial force endowed with the unrestricted power of will. This Divine Being, according to tantrics, permeates every aspect of creation. What prevents us from experiencing its presence is our own ignorance, which stands like a wall between individual and universal consciousness. The tantric method of mantra sadhana is one of the surest ways to demolish that wall and experience God the way She is.

The key element in practicing mantra in a tantric manner is to establish a personal relationship with its power. This takes place only after intense practices resulting in the tantric adepts having a direct, intuitive experience of the *ishta deva*, the personified form of the mantra they are practicing. This form is the actual materialization of the mantric energy, not a product of imagination. The ancients literally saw the personified form of the mantra, just as we see tangible objects in our daily life, and when they described the physical counterpart of the mantric energy in minute detail, the vision served to open the way for dedicated practitioners to have *darshana*, or a glimpse, of the mantra. This is how the concept of deities developed in tantra.

Cultivating love and respect for the mantra is more important than concentration on the mantra—but establishing a relationship with something which is solely auditory, and therefore merely conceptual, is difficult for most people. It is not difficult, however, to feel the presence of the Divine when the sense of sight is involved. We are accustomed to experiencing shape, color, and texture, and the personified forms of the deities described by adepts are accompanied by all these familiar elements of cognition. We can relate to them. Thus in tantric practice mantra becomes a tool not only for focusing the mind but also for filling the mind with the grace of the deity. We can now cultivate a personal relationship with the deity corresponding to the mantra we are practicing, convincing ourselves intellectually that the mantra and the deity are one and the same and that we are communicating with Her with each repetition. This is where an understanding of tantric metaphysics becomes important.

Every religion perceives God in a distinct form, and if we have been raised in a particular religion we have a natural preference for that form over any other. Practicing a mantra in a tantric manner, however, involves meditating on the form of a deity, and this can conflict with our religious upbringing. So it is best therefore not to undertake such a practice until we understand tantric metaphysics, which describe the interrelationship of sound and light. Modern science and technology have made it relatively easy for us to understand how light signals are translated into sound and vice versa. The next step is to understand how sound and light relate with the energy that transcends the physical realm. When we grasp this we will understand how a mantra can have a personified form, we will comprehend the inner meaning of this form, and we will realize that meditating on it in conjunction with reciting its mantra has nothing to do with religion.

In tantrism every mantra or group of mantras is associated with a specific deity—the deity is the visual form of the mantra; the mantra is the auditory form of the deity. The vibratory patterns of the mantras are associated with different levels of forces both within us and within the cosmos, and the deities are the archetypes of those forces. The light of the Divine itself manifests in the form of mantra. Thus each mantra is a focus of light, and intense meditation on a mantra enables us to see it as light in the personified form of the deity. Knowing what can be known about the form of the deity that corresponds to the mantra helps us intensify our feelings during the practice.

Gayatri

FREE GAYATRI MANTRA MP3

In tantra sadhana the correct pronunciation of the mantra is crucial for the success of the practice. For that reason we are making available a MP3 of Pandit Rajmani Tigunait teaching how to recite the Gayatri mantra and how to practice it in a tantric manner. This involves reciting specific mantras, invoking the guru lineage, purifying the atmosphere and the meditation seat, imbuing one's heart with the power of the mantra, and synchronizing the energy of the mantra with various limbs and organs of the body. Download at HimalayanInstitute.org/Gayatri

The medium of communication at the level of feeling is blocked if the deity is beyond our reach. Some of us can override our cultural conditioning, but most of us cannot. And so to overcome the sense of separateness caused by ignorance of our oneness with the Divine, tantrics include complementary practices in their mantra sadhana. Two major components of such practices are *prana pratistha* and *nyasa*.

Prana pratistha is an intense visualization, and it is further energized by the mantra. It causes you to feel that the deity is sitting in the lotus of your heart, or even that you have been replaced, and the meditation about to be undertaken is actually being done by the deity. This helps you rise above the dualistic consciousness which led you to believe that you and the primordial life-force were two different entities.

Next comes *nyasa*, which means "to synchronize different aspects of the mantra with different aspects of our being." This practice helps you to synchronize the forces of the mantra with the different limbs and organs of your body. There are different levels of nyasa practice. At the first stage of initiation a simple version is used. (In the practice of the highest category of tantric mantras, such as Sri Vidya, the nyasa is quite elaborate.) In this simple version the mantra is divided into six parts and is established in the thumbs, index fingers, middle fingers, ring fingers, little fingers, and palms through the power of concentration. This is called *kara nyasa*, synchronization of the mantra's power with the energies of the hands. Next comes *anga nyasa:* synchronization of the six parts of the mantra with the energies of the heart, the head, the crown of the head, the chest and shoulders, the three eyes, and the space pervaded by the pranic body. The final step, known as *vyapaka nyasa*, involves synchronizing the energy of the mantra with the entire body.

THE TANTRIC METHOD OF PRACTICING GAYATRI

To further clarify this tantric form of mantra practice let us return to the gayatri mantra, one of the most famous mantras in the Vedas. This mantra has a maternal quality. It guides us in the right direction and warns us at a subtle level when we are about to make a mistake. And if mistakes have already been made, the gayatri mantra lovingly corrects them. The mantra is: *Om bhur bhuvah svah tat savitur vareniyam bhargo devasya dhimahi dhiyo yo nah prachodayat.*

In the ordinary course of meditation on gayatri all you have to do is sit with your head, neck, and trunk in a straight line, relax your body, breathe gently and smoothly, and bring your attention to the center suggested by your teacher (such as the navel, heart, or eyebrow center) and remember the mantra. The tantric method is much more elaborate. The most comprehensive method consists of completing auxiliary practices known as *sandhyopasana*, the twilight meditation, before doing *japa* (repetition) of the gayatri mantra. A shorter version consists of invoking the guru lineage, purifying the atmosphere and your seat with special mantras, and drawing an imaginary wall of fire around you to protect yourself from external influences.

Prana Pratistha

Prana pratistha means "invoking the deity and imbuing one's heart with that energy." While placing the palms over the heart, the aspirant meditates on the personified form of the deity at the heart center while reciting the following mantra:

Om am hrim krom yam ram lam vam sham sham sam ham hamsah so ham mama hridaye bhagavati gayatri ihaivagatya sukham chiram tishthatu svaha. Om om om pratistha.

Kara Nyasa and Anga Nyasa

This is followed by the simple version of nyasa. Before you begin, it is important to know that "Om bhur bhuvah svah" is not part of the original gayatri mantra. This particular segment is called *vyahriti* (the covering) and always accompanies the mantra. Excluding this covering, the gayatri mantra consists of twenty-four syllables. To synchronize the mantra with the body, it is split into six parts, each containing four syllables:

1. tatsavituh

2. vareniyam

3. bhargo deva

4. syadhimahi

5. dhiyo yo nah

6. prachodayat

These six parts of the mantra are synchronized with the thumbs, index fingers, middle fingers, ring fingers, little fingers, and the palms. During the practice you repeat one segment of the mantra enveloped by *Om bhur bhuvah svah* while concentrating on the corresponding limb or organ. Here is how it is done:

1. *Om bhur bhuvah svah tatsavituh*
   Om bhur bhuvah svah angusthabhyam namah (thumbs)

2. *Om bhur bhuvah svah vareniyam*
   Om bhur bhuvah svah tarjanibhyam svaha (index fingers)

3. Om *bhur bhuvah svah bhargo deva*
   Om *bhur bhuvah svah madhyamabhyam vashat*
   (middle fingers)

4. Om *bhur bhuvah svah syadhimahi*
   Om *bhur bhuvah svah anamikabhyam hum*
   (ring fingers)

5. Om *bhur bhuvah svah dhiyo yo nah*
   Om *bhur bhuvah svah kanisthikabhyam vaushat*
   (little fingers)

6. Om *bhur bhuvah svah prachodayat*
   Om *bhur bhuva svah karatala pristhabhyam phat*
   (palms)

This is immediately followed by *anga nyasa*:

1. Om *bhur bhuva svah tatsavituh*
   Om *bhur bhuva svah hridaya namah* (heart)

2. Om *bhur bhuva svah vareniyam*
   Om *bhur bhuva svah shirase svaha* (head)

3. Om *bhur bhuva svah bhargo deva*
   Om *bhur bhuva svah shikhayai vashat*
   (crown of the head)

4. Om *bhur bhuva svah syadhimahi*
   Om *bhur bhuva svah kavachaya hum*
   (chest and shoulders)

5. *Om bhur bhuva svah dhiyo yo nah*
   Om bhur bhuva svah netratrayaya vaushat (eyes)

6. *Om bhur bhuva svah prachodayat*
   Om bhur bhuva svah astrya phat
   (the space pervaded by the pranic body)

Vyapaka Nyasa

The final step is to synchronize the energy of the mantra with the entire body. Vyapaka nyasa is this process. It lets the power of mantra pervade the entire body, thereby creating perfect harmony between mantra and practitioner. This practice is done by meditating on the personified form of Gayatri, the deity of the mantra, in the space occupied by the body, or by meditating on fire in the place of the body while repeating the entire gayatri mantra: *Om bhur bhuvah svah tat savitur vareniyam bhargo devasya dhimahi dhiyo yo nah prachodayat.* If the meditation is intense you feel as though the mantra is vibrating simultaneously from every limb and organ of the body of the Goddess. If you are meditating on fire during the vyapaka nyasa, synchronize the sound of the mantra with the movement of the flames. Thus you feel that your whole body (which has been replaced either by the deity or by the fire) is filled with the power of mantra.

MANTRA JAPA

After you have done vyapaka nyasa, you begin to recite the entire mantra *(mantra japa)*. In tantric practice this is very methodical—you must do a certain amount of *japa* (the repetition of a mantra) every day. The complementary practices just described are used only for the gayatri mantra—other mantras have their own complementary practices.

Once you have become familiar with the mantra and its complementary practices, the teacher designs a definite course of practice for you: a *purascharana* (*purascharana* means "taking the first step"), which involves doing a specific amount of japa in a defined period of time. The shortest purascharana of the gayatri mantra, for example, requires 125,000 repetitions in 125 days. To do this you must use mala beads, a "necklace" consisting of 108 beads which you hold in one hand and use as a counter: one bead for each repetition of the mantra. When you complete one round, you have done 108 repetitions, but only 100 are counted; the remaining eight are automatically dedicated to Ganesha, the remover of obstacles (see chapter 5).

The standard course of japa for a purascharana is 2.4 million repetitions. If you do 100 malas a day it takes eight months to complete that purascharana; if you do 50 malas a day it takes sixteen months; 25 malas, 32 months. If you undertake the standard course and are doing 100 or 50 malas a day you must stay in one place, preferably one that is free from worldly distractions. (The scriptures consider a shrine, a hilltop, a monastery, or an ashram of an accomplished yogi most conducive to mantra sadhana.) You must also follow strict dietary observances throughout the practice and take care not to associate with people who distract you from your spiritual focus.

Not everyone can adhere to the restrictions necessary to a gayatri purascharana at the rate of 100 or 50 malas of gayatri per day, but even so it is best to complete the practice as quickly as possible. If you are doing only 25 malas a day you do not have to stay in one place for the 32 months it will take to complete the purascharana, but you will need to preserve your energy in thought, speech, and action. You must refrain from psychoactive drugs, alcohol, and meat, and practice *brahmacharya* (celibacy) if possible, or at least stay within the confines of marital life. Austerities that help you preserve your energy and allow your internal fire to glow are called *tapas*. Practically speaking, *tapas* means "discipline." The more disciplined you are, the more intense your practice.

During the purascharana, each time you sit to do your japa you must begin with the complementary practices. Suppose that you have to get up in the middle of the practice for some reason. When you resume you must do the complementary practices again, because unless you synchronize the forces of mantra with the energies of your body and mind the japa will remain dry and mechanical. It is through the oneness between you and the mantra shakti, a oneness established through the complementary practices, that you find joy in doing japa. Without this experience your practice will be a chore. This attitude invites boredom, which in turn undermines your determination, making it unlikely that you will complete the purascharana.

After the course of japa is completed the teacher may prescribe a fire offering of certain grains, herbs, and clarified butter. It is usually made one-tenth as many times as the mantra has been repeated. In other words if you have done 125,000 repetitions of the gayatri mantra you make 12,500 offerings into the fire, and with each offering you repeat the mantra, adding "svaha" at the end just as you are about to offer the oblation into the fire. In many traditions, however, the fire offering is substituted by meditation on the navel center, in which you visualize fire at that center and repeat the gayatri mantra followed by "svaha."

EXPERIENCE AS THE TEACHER

Tantric mantras can be extremely potent, and many do not have the benign and loving qualities of gayatri. That is why they must be received from a teacher and practiced according to strict guidelines. The adepts know exactly how much energy should be unleashed and how to contain and assimilate that energy. We are accustomed to thinking that if something is good, then more is better. In tantra sadhana this kind of thinking can be injurious.

I will cite my own experience. One September just before he left for India my gurudeva gave me the practice of a particular variety of gayatri called Ganesha Gayatri, instructing me to complete it in thirty-three days. Because of my hectic travel schedule I kept postponing the practice because I could not find an interval of thirty-three days when I would be in the same place. I very much wanted to complete the practice before Swamiji returned from India in March, so I came up with a plan. There were two weeks in January when I was not traveling, and I decided to go into silence during that period and speed up the practice so I could complete it in eleven days instead of thirty-three.

There was a hitch, however: on one of the weekends when I would be doing the practice I had also to give a lecture. I told the other faculty members that I would be observing silence with the exception of an hour and a half on Saturday evening, and asked if I could be scheduled to lecture then. Everyone agreed.

I began my practice in Swamiji's cabin, and my wife brought me food once a day. One day along with lunch she brought a note from the seminar coordinator asking if I could lecture Saturday morning instead of Saturday evening. I wrote that I could. But the next day my wife brought another note, this one asking if I would agree to return to the original schedule. Again I agreed. At noon on Saturday my wife received a third note, this one asking me to postpone my lecture until Sunday morning. This was too much: I lost my temper—but because I was in silence there was no way to express my anger. My hand shaking in rage, I wrote: "Anytime is fine with me; just let me know when."

After my wife left, a torrent of emotions flooded my mind. I could not stop thinking, "This person is deliberately trying to disturb me. Once this practice is over I'm going to teach her a lesson!" I was so disturbed that I could no longer concentrate. Normally it took fifteen minutes for me to complete one round on my mala, but after thirty minutes I was not even halfway through. An hour later I got up and took a bath, hoping it would calm me down. It didn't. Throughout the afternoon and into the early evening I struggled—barely managing to complete two rounds, something I could normally do in thirty minutes. Now I was afraid I wouldn't be able to complete the practice in eleven days.

Then I remembered that ever since I was a child I had been in the habit of looking to the *Ramayana*, an epic about the life of Rama, for answers whenever I needed help. So I picked up a copy, closed my eyes, and opened it at random. The verse read: "How can those who are fully surrendered to Rama (and as a result are free from desire, ego, greed, and anger) and those who see Rama in everyone and everything have any animosity toward anyone?" Instantly I realized that I had not fully surrendered to the Divine, and that is why I was not free from anger. Furthermore, I was not seeing the Divine in the woman who was sending me the notes, and this was why I had been suffering from animosity toward her. The realization calmed me down immediately, and I was able to resume my practice.

I completed it on the eleventh day, so exhausted that when I finished the last repetition of the mantra I leaned against the chair behind my meditation seat and slipped into a reverie-like state. I saw an old sage sitting on the couch in front of me. In my heart I felt that he was Swamiji's master, and out of respect I got up and put my head on his feet. He looked at me lovingly and said, "I am glad that you completed the practice." Then he extended his cupped hand, on which a seed rested. "Do you see this seed?" he asked. "By consuming a certain amount of light, heat, water, and nutrients within a certain length of time, it sprouts, grows, flowers, and finally bears fruit. If you provide all the light, heat, water, and nutrients in a concentrated period, what will happen to this poor seed? It will roast or it will rot. I am happy you did the practice, but . . ." With that he disappeared, and I found myself sitting next to the couch instead of leaning against the chair.

Because tantric sadhana is a way of reweaving the fabric of life, before we undertake it we must familiarize ourselves not only with the pattern in the fabric but also with the nature of the threads. The more advanced the practice, the greater the need for knowing accurately the intensity of the currents and crosscurrents of the waves of energy traveling in our body. That is why tantric masters so often ignore their students' requests for practices.

I learned this lesson in 1976, when during the Kumbha Mela in Allahabad I met an adept, Swami Sanatan Deva Ji Maharaj, the disciple of the great master Devarahawa Baba (popularly known as "the ageless sage"). This saint impressed me both with his kindness and with his yogic accomplishments, so one day after some time had passed I asked him to bless me with *shaktipata* (the direct transmission of spiritual energy). For a while he ignored my request. Then, pointing at my chest, he said, "You have some old injuries, and your internal organs will not be able to carry the strong currents of energy induced by such a high level of initiation." I was awed by his capacity for intuitive diagnosis: eight years earlier, while still recovering from typhoid fever I had injured my chest while racing to jump onto a moving train.

Masters make sure that we have met the prerequisites before they initiate us into the higher practices. That is why the first level of kaula practices consists of replacing our sense of self with an awareness of the deity and synchronizing the power of the mantra with different limbs and organs of the body. This demolishes the wall of duality by aligning the power of the mantra and the dynamic forces of the body with those of the cosmos. And this in turn creates an internal environment in which we draw closer to the Divinity and establish a firm seat at the base of Her pedestal. The scriptures call this process *upasana*, "sitting close." In fact the first level of tantric initiation *is* upasana, for it enables us to experience our intimate relationship with the personified form of the deity. It is true that this and the practices that follow are grounded in duality, but they give us the ability to experience the Divine Mother manifesting in all names and forms. To further deepen our understanding the adepts grant the next level of initiation when we are ready.

Chapter Five

THE SECOND INITIATION: YANTRA

We have seen that initiation into mantra sadhana and our subsequent engagement with the accompanying practices gives us an opportunity to bask in the presence of the primordial life-force known to tantrics as the Divine Mother. We have also seen that, through prolonged mantra sadhana, an increasingly intimate relationship develops between the practitioner and the mantric energy. And as this intimacy matures, an urge arises to explore the intricacies of this relationship to a greater degree. That is when we are ready to be initiated into yantra.

Yantra sadhana is the natural extension of mantra sadhana, and in a strict sense kaula tantric practice begins here. Mantra initiation enables us to recognize our relationship with the Divine Mother, but it does not necessarily help us experience either Her relationship with the dynamic forces that emanate from Her or our own relationship with those forces. This is the fruit of meditating on a yantra.

The deity is not the only visual form of the mantra. Mantric energy also takes a visual form known as yantra, a geometrical diagram (perceived intuitively by the sages in the course of their inward journey) which reveals complex interrelationships between the meditator and the Divine Mother: the sound of the mantra is accompanied by the same vibratory patterns in yantric form. In other words, like the personified form of the deity, yantras are visible expressions of the mantric rays. Just as the nuclear activity in the sun engenders the heat and light that radiates outward, so does the inherent creativity of the Divine Mother radiate outward in the form of mantras (sound) and yantras (light). To those of us who have not gained access to the Divine the patterns formed by the mantric rays remain imperceptible; so to guide us to the realm beyond mind and senses the sages have mapped the mantric world in the form of yantras. By following this map we not only draw nearer to the Divine Force, we also begin to experience its dynamic interplay with the mantric energy of the yantra.

Tantric sadhana is long and difficult, and for this reason the first and fundamental practice is to meditate on a yantra that will help us remove all of the obstacles that may arise during the more advanced practices. Most of these, the tantric masters have observed, are associated with concerns and issues that correspond to the two lowest chakras. For example the obstacles of fear, insecurity, sloth, inertia, and dullness are associated with the first chakra; those of desire, attachment, anger, lust, and all forms of sensual urges are associated with the second. Most of our diseases, both physical and psychological, constitute further obstacles; they have their origins in issues related to these two chakras. The obstacles of depression, grief, and a lack of self-motivation are caused by disturbances at these two chakras.

All of these forces wreak havoc on the spiritual journey and have to be brought under control if we hope to succeed. We must be healthy and strong at the physical level, and stable at the emotional level. Intellectual clarity and sharpness is of utmost importance. When we have cultivated an indomitable will and the power of determination that accompanies it we will face fewer obstacles, and we will have the ability to overcome those we do encounter. For all of these reasons adepts first initiate their students into the Ganesha yantra, a special sadhana that removes all obstacles.

THE SIGNIFICANCE OF GANESHA

The Divine Mother assumes infinite names and forms, each of which expresses a different facet of Her being. The deity Ganesha, Her first-born son, is a case in point. *Ganesha* is a compound of the Sanskrit words *gana* and *isha*. *Gana* means "individual beings, independent units, segments of light, discrete bodies of Divinity, unique forces, emanations of Divine Light, attendants of the main deity." *Isha* means "one who is capable of doing what he wishes, capable of refraining from what he does not wish to do, and capable of undoing that which has already been done"—in short, the Almighty Lord.

Ganesha dwells eternally in the womb of the Divine Mother. He is the "firstborn one," emerging from Her before any of the functioning forces of the universe emerge. In their manifest form all these forces center around this primordial force—Ganesha is the locus for all that exists. He establishes law and brings order out of chaos, causing the universal forces to function coherently.

The first step in bringing order out of chaos is the emergence of the law of gravity, and Ganesha is the presiding deity of that law. At his behest the force of gravity captures all the matter and energy emitted by the primordial Divine Force and gives direction to its outward movement. Ganesha himself is the center of all gravitational energy, and as such he supervises all activities, from the microcosm to the macrocosm—everything in the universe is held by the invisible strings of

gravity, while gravity itself is held by Ganesha. The forces of
creation, maintenance, and destruction are held in harmonious balance by his will, and that is why this firstborn child
of the Divine Mother is called "Ganesha," the lord of all
entities and functioning forces of the universe.

According to the chakra scheme of kundalini yoga,
Ganesha resides in the first chakra, the *muladhara*. *Mula*
means "original, main"; *adhara* means "base, foundation."
From the standpoint of manifestation, or outward expansion
of the primordial Divine Force, the muladhara chakra is the
principle on which everything rests. In his visual form at the
muladhara center, Ganesha is described as an enormous man
with the head of an elephant. He is heavy and strong, capable
of crushing obstacles into dust. Seated at the base of the spine
he holds, supports, and guides all other chakras, thus governing the forces that propel the wheel of life.

To understand the symbolic meaning of Ganesha's
personality we have to examine his personified form. Half
human and half elephant, he represents human intelligence
wedded to the strength of an elephant. The parts of his body
are disproportionate: he has big ears, small eyes, a long trunk,
a massive belly, and small feet. He is paradox embodied:
although he is enormous, his vehicle is a mouse; he consumes
huge quantities of food, yet he is an ascetic; he is fat and his
legs are short, yet he is master of the dance.

His boundless intelligence is symbolized by his big head.
The epithet given to him in both Vedic and tantric scriptures
is Brahmanaspati, "lord of knowledge and intelligence" or "lord
of pervasiveness." The scriptures also refer to him as Jyeshtha
Raja, "the eldest son," even though he was never born.

Ganesha's massive belly symbolizes his capacity to
consume and contain the universe that evolves from the
Divine Mother. As the lord of gravitational energy he has the

Ganesha

capacity to pull anything toward himself and process it as he wishes. He also sets the wheel of karma in motion. That is why the scriptures describe him as Karma Adhyaksha, "the one who presides over karmic law."

Ganesha is immortal. In him lies the seed of omniscience, and the most subtle mysteries of the universe are known to him, including the mysteries related to our mind, karma, and the cycle of birth and death. The rays of light emanating from him enable us to comprehend our deeply rooted karmic impressions and discover how to attain freedom from the binding forces of our mind. Only then are the obstacles emerging from its unlit corners fully destroyed. Hence he is called Vighnesha, "the lord who removes obstacles."

Like fire, Ganesha consumes anything in his path with his enormous appetite. He is pleased with any offering we make to him with love—he gladly accepts our problems and concerns and swallows them, granting us freedom once and for all. No force other than Ganesha is capable of consuming our ignorance, egoism, attachment, aversion, and fear of death. That is also why he is called Vighnesha, "the lord who removes obstacles."

His big ears symbolize his limitless capacity for hearing. He hears our prayers regardless of how we recite them—he does not care whether or not we sing hymns in his praise, he considers our heartbeat and brainwaves to be forms of prayer. Any irregularity, whatever the cause, catches his attention. Being Ganesha, the head of the family, he rushes to our rescue. For these reasons, too, he is known as Vighnesha, "the lord who removes obstacles."

The fluid that sometimes flows from the temporal gland of male elephants flows constantly from Ganesha, and drawn by its sweet aroma insects drink the nectar. Intoxicated, they buzz around his ears, which he flaps gently in order to ward them off. This tells us metaphorically that Ganesha's head, the treasure-house of wisdom, is so filled with the sweetness of love and compassion that it flows from him effortlessly and incessantly and is granted even to those who come to him with a noisy mind.

Set in his enormous head, Ganesha's eyes are small because he has little use for them. However his third eye, the eye of intuition, is wide open, and he sees past, present, and future simultaneously. Seated as he is deep within every living and non-living entity, he sees everything. That is why he is called Adi Rishi, "the primordial seer." He is the eternal source of knowledge—revelation flows through him. The scriptures refer to him as Parama Guru, "the master of all previous masters."

The scriptures identify Ganesha with the sacred sound Om, and the shape of his trunk resembles the word written in Sanskrit. Because Om is the source of all mantras, repeating any mantra is tantamount to meditating on Ganesha. All sounds, words, and mantras in their dormant form rest in the muladhara chakra, where Ganesha resides.

The most subtle, vibrationless state of sound in the muladhara chakra is called "para." At the behest of Ganesha, who presides over gravitational energy, a stirring arises in the muladhara chakra that can be detected only intuitively. This vibrationless vibration can be felt when it reaches the navel center; when it reaches the heart center, it assimilates the power of thinking; and it becomes audible when it reaches the throat center. Ganesha oversees this entire process. Without his assistance and guidance we can neither gain access to the muladhara center nor receive the ensuing revelation. That is why Ganesha is said to be the gatekeeper at the palace of the Divine Mother.

Though Ganesha's feet are quite small, he outruns all the forces of the universe—because he pervades everything, he is

already everywhere. Without moving, the lord of gravitational energy makes everything move. With his enormous
body and tiny feet Ganesha dances to the song of the Divine
Mother, and exhilarated by his movements, She joins in.
Then, as mother and son perform their cosmic dance, all the
arts and sciences spring forth. Unable to contain the divine
ecstasy, the sages emerge from their absorption in Ganesha
and assume their roles as our guides. This cosmic dance symbolizes the process of kundalini awakening. The forces of
darkness can cast their spell of slumber on us only as long as
we are outside the pale of this dance. Thus Ganesha, the
remover of obstacles, is the one who awakens the divine
force in the form of kundalini shakti. He blesses us with
shaktipata (the bestowing of divine energy). It is he who
sends a *sat guru* (a true master) into our lives, and through
his grace the forces of love, compassion, self-motivation,
self-confidence, and determination unfold. Thus the scriptures assert that the door to the Divine Mother's palace
opens when Ganesha is pleased.

There are hundreds of ways to propitiate Ganesha and
meditate on him. The tantric method, in conjunction with
yantra sadhana, is precise and methodical. Those whose prolonged practice has gained them access to the muladhara
center meditate on Ganesha by practicing the tantric
method of kundalini yoga. To them, the human body is a
yantra. Others draw the yantra of Ganesha on a gold, silver,
or copper plate, on a silk cloth, on a wooden board, or on a
piece of birch bark, and meditate on that.

THE GANESHA YANTRA

Except for the circle in the center, the Ganesha yantra
consists of three circuits. The following description is found in
the *Prapancha Sara,* a scripture attributed to Shankaracharya.

Om

Ganesha resides in the central circle, accompanied by a cluster of shaktis (forces, or powers). He is seated on a mouse, a small creature that is nevertheless powerful enough to carry him. The mouse is the embodiment of nine forces:

1. The power of intensity *(tivra)*

2. The power of radiance *(jvalini)*

3. The power of delight *(nanda)*

4. The power that gives pleasure *(bhogada)*

5. The power of desire *(kamarupini)*

6. The power of speed *(ugra)*

7. The power of illumination *(tejovati)*

8. The power of being *(satya)*

9. The power that destroys resistance *(vighna vinashini)*

In tantric terminology these nine forces are collectively called *pitha shakti* (the forces that constitute Ganesha's seat). They are Ganesha's own emanations, which he uses to localize himself in the space of pure consciousness. His two intrinsic forces, *buddhi* (the power of intelligence) and *siddhi* (the power of success), accompany him on his right and left, respectively. The powers of intelligence and success are the dynamic aspect of Ganesha, while he himself represents the static aspect.

Ganesha yantra

Outside this circle reside four pairs of shaktis, one pair in each of the four directions: north, east, south, and west. They represent:

1. The dynamic and static power of sustenance
   (Rama and Ramesha)

2. The dynamic and static power of stability
   (Mahi and Varaha)

3. The dynamic and static power of renovation and
   restructuring (Uma and Maheshvara)

4. The dynamic and static power of love and attraction
   (Rati and Kamadeva)

These four pairs of forces are direct emanations of Ganesha, which he uses to govern and guide all sentient and insentient beings in creation. The forces of sustenance, stability, renovation/restructuring, and attraction work in perfect coordination and harmony.

When the world is on the brink of collapse, the dynamic and static power of sustenance (Rama and Ramesha, also known as Vishnu and Lakshmi) come forward to maintain and preserve it. When destructive forces become dominant and threaten to overpower the forces of sustenance, the power of stability takes over. It is said that whenever the ecosystem is imbalanced and the earth is suffocating, Varaha (the power of stability in the form of a boar) incarnates, restores stability, and brings law and order to the planet earth, known as Mahi. Thus the planet earth and the boar symbolize the dynamic and static power of stability.

The first circuit

When ecological imbalance worsens, then Ganesha commissions his next level of emanation, the power of renovation and restructuring. Renovation is always preceded by demolition, and for this reason the dynamic and static forces of renovation and restructuring are referred to as Uma and Maheshvara (or Shakti and Shiva). But the forces of love and attraction, Rati and Kamadeva, always accompany the first three pairs. Therefore the entire process of creation, sustenance, stability, renovation, and restructuring is held together by the dynamic and static power of love and attraction. That is why this world, with all its diversities, its pains and pleasures, its ups and downs, appears to be so beautiful. The following six pairs of shaktis reside in the second circuit:

1. The dynamic and static power of worldly and spiritual prosperity (Riddhi and Amoda)

2. The dynamic and static power of worldly and spiritual enjoyment (Samriddhi and Pramoda)

3. The dynamic and static power of intoxication (Mada-drava and Avighnesha)

4. The dynamic and static power of desire and indulgence (Madanavati and Durmukha)

5. The dynamic and static power of liquefaction (Dravani and Vighnakarta)

6. The dynamic and static power of beautification (Kanti and Sumukha)

The second circuit

These six pairs of forces are extremely important in both our worldly and spiritual endeavors, for we experience true success only when they work in harmony. The first pair of shaktis, the power of prosperity, refers to abundance—but abundance is meaningless if we do not know how to use it (many prosperous people are insecure and fearful misers). Hence the fortune brought by this first pair of forces is further invested and multiplied by the second pair of shaktis, the power of worldly and spiritual enjoyment: this pair enables us to use and enjoy inner and outer prosperity to its fullest.

The third pair of shaktis, roughly translated as the power of intoxication, helps us find joy in seeing others benefit from our prosperity. The name of the dynamic form of this shakti is Mada-drava, "the one who melts due to her own inherent joy," because she is intoxicated by her own overflowing love and compassion. Because of this shakti we find joy in sharing the wealth bestowed upon us by the first two forces. This particular force removes the obstacles to our spiritual growth caused by worldly success.

The fourth pair of shaktis, the power of desire and indulgence, forces us to become attached to our achievements. It fattens our ego, causing us to suffer from vanity. We begin to seek recognition from outside, which consequently weakens our sense of self-respect and self-appreciation. We do not find ourselves beautiful any more, and so we try to hide this self-created ugliness under a mask of vanity. That is why the static aspect of this pair is known as Durmukha, "the ugly-faced one."

The fifth pair of shaktis, the power of liquefaction, causes us to find satisfaction in seeing others melt away. This pair always works in coordination with the fourth and becomes a source of obstacles, and these obstacles become stronger if the fifth pair of shaktis is disconnected from the third pair. That is why the static aspect of this power is called Vighnakarta, "the creator of obstacles," while the static aspect of the third power is known as Avighnesha, "the remover of obstacles."

The sixth shakti, the power of beautification, helps us identify with our inherent beauty and bliss. Because of the way this shakti functions we do not seek appreciation from outside: we love and respect ourselves for whatever we are; we are self-content and self-contained. The energy emitted by our inner beauty and bliss is so compelling that not only do we experience ourselves as beautiful, but others also experience our beauty. That is why the static aspect of this power is called Sumukha, "the beautiful-faced one" in contrast to the static aspect of the fourth shakti, "the ugly-faced one."

Our well-rounded growth depends on the balanced functioning of these six pairs of shaktis. Seated in the center of the yantra, Ganesha pulls the strings, disturbing or reestablishing equilibrium among them. Tantrics believe that ordinarily one of these pairs dominates the others, causing us to ride the roller coaster of prosperity and poverty, compassion and cruelty, overindulgence and repression. We continue being tossed by the pairs of opposites until one day we receive the guidance and protection from Ganesha's two intrinsic forces: buddhi and siddhi, the power of intelligence and the power of success. Two pairs of shaktis reside in the third and final circuit of the yantra:

1. The dynamic and static aspects of the power that keeps our inner and outer wealth in flux (Vasudhara and Shankhanidhi)

2. The dynamic and static aspects of the power that keeps our wealth stable (Vasumati and Padmanidhi)

These two pairs of shaktis encircle the second circuit. The first pair of shaktis initiates change, causing a dormant force to become active; the second pair engenders stability. They symbolize the fact that all forces inside the yantra are embraced simultaneously by the laws of transitoriness and eternity. Both pairs of shaktis must work in complete coordination with each other. If change is not tempered by stability, chaos ensues; if stability is not tempered by change, stagnation sets in. The purpose of life is accomplished somewhere between these two extremes.

UNDERTAKING THE PRACTICE

The exact method of entering the yantra, reaching the central circle, and propitiating Ganesha and his intrinsic shaktis (the powers of intelligence and success) is not clearly described in any one place. Instead instructions are scattered throughout a number of scriptures and are somewhat contradictory, so that even after studying various texts it is impossible to know how to do this practice correctly. Anyone aspiring to do this sadhana must find a teacher who is an initiate of a living tradition who has studied and practiced under the guidance of a master.

Tradition dictates that if you find such a master, he or she will first initiate you into the Ganesha mantra and the auxiliary practices. Then, when this first level of your sadhana is complete, the master will determine whether or not you are ready to receive the second level of tantra initiation: initiation into the Ganesha yantra. As a part of this the teacher will introduce you to the set of mantras that are used in meditating on different aspects of the yantra. The success of this sadhana depends on practicing precise methods of visualization and performing rituals in exact accordance with the rules laid down by the tradition. If done correctly this practice

The third circuit

engenders strength and stability at both the physical and emotional levels, and it will unfold intellectual clarity and sharpness, a prerequisite for cultivating an indomitable will. From the power of determination comes the wisdom and strength to use the four primitive urges (food, sex, sleep, and self-preservation) in a purposeful manner.

Thus the experience gained from completing this second level of practice will make you decisive and fearless. Now you are ready to undertake any tantric sadhana—be it associated with higher levels of yantra sadhana or the practice of chakra puja (left-hand tantra)—because you will be under the guidance and protection of the master of all previous masters, Ganesha himself, who resides in the muladhara chakra and presides over all forces of body and mind. The doors to all tantra practices are now completely open to you—nothing is forbidden to you any more.

Chapter Six

THE THIRD INITIATION: CHAKRA PUJA

*T*he first two levels of initiation within the kaula school of tantra help us unveil the mystery of the right-hand path. The left-hand disciplines constitute the final stage of the sadhana, but this initiation is conferred only after the preliminary practices have been completed and the master has found, after repeated testing, that the student has no craving for sense gratification and upholds the sacredness of the left-hand path.

Each stage of kaula sadhana depends upon the one before it. After the first initiation, for example, we have to complete a well-defined course of mantra sadhana, known as *purascharana*, which helps us experience our relationship with the Divine Mother, and it is only after we have completed this practice that we are qualified to receive the second initiation. Yantra sadhana, the next level of practice, brings us into direct con-tact with the multi-layered forces within the microcosm and the macrocosm that lie beyond our normal realm of con-sciousness. At this level of initiation, yantra sadhana is accompanied by rituals, visualization, contemplation, mantra recitation, and fire offerings. The principles of self-restraint and specific disciplines—cultivating a strong and healthy body, practicing breathing exercises, eating vegetarian meals, observing silence, curtailing sleep, bathing at least twice a day, and refraining from excessive socializing—play an important role in this sadhana. Adhering to these disciplines familiarizes us with our strengths and weaknesses, and in the process we gain considerable control over our primitive urges. But even though we attain the ability to subdue our subhuman tendencies, their subtle traces are still hidden somewhere deep in our unconscious. And tantrics believe that as long as this is the case there is always a possibility that we will come under their influence.

It is true that the practices of the first two levels of initiation help us acknowledge our subhuman tendencies. However when taken to an extreme—eating too little, sleeping too little, depriving ourselves of company and all forms of entertainment—these observances sap our vitality and create the illusion that we have attained freedom from the cravings of the senses. Left-hand tantrics poke fun at this. They use the analogy of a horse race: you have a strong, healthy horse, but it has not been trained and you do not know how to ride; the cinch is loose and you have only a feeble grip on the reins— and yet you are in a race. After falling off and hurting yourself repeatedly, you decide that the horse is too strong and conclude that the only way you will ever win the race is if the horse is weak enough for you to control it.

According to left-hand tantrics, this is silly and self-defeating. The horse is the senses; the mind the reins. You can win the race for spiritual and worldly success only by nourishing and training your senses. You must also have a good grip on the reins, which is possible only if you have sharpened your intellect and cultivated your power of will and determination. During the early training period (the first two initiations) you may need a horse you can dominate, one that is not bursting with energy that you have no skill to control. But to win the race you must have a strong, healthy horse and the ability to control it. Gaining this mastery is the goal of left-hand kaula practices.

Tantrics that follow the left-hand path live in the world, enjoy it to its fullest, and yet remain above it. Their disciplines make sure they will have a strong, healthy body and mind and that their intellect will be crystal-clear so they can detect the deceptive behaviors of their mind and senses. And because they know the pitfalls on this path they center their sadhana around the master, from whom they never conceal anything. In fact one key guideline on this path is: "Do not assume that your master is a great and enlightened sage and therefore knows all about you. Even if he knows, it is still your duty to tell him your weaknesses. But there is no need to tell him your strengths."

THE LEFT-HAND PATH

Left-hand tantric practice is traditionally known as *chakra puja*, "worshipping the chakras." Here the word *chakra* has a double meaning: a chakra is a center of consciousness within the body, and a chakra is also a circle—in this context it is a circle formed by a group of practitioners. The human body is the living shrine and the chakras are altars within that shrine. The practice of sitting in a circle around the master while worshipping the Divine Force at the altar of the chakras is called chakra puja. The master is known as *chakreshvara* (the lord of the chakras and the lord of the circle of aspirants). In other words, instead of invoking the Divine in a geometrical yantra, left-hand tantrics invoke Her in the yantra of the human body.

According to left-hand tantrics the Divine Force resides in the muladhara chakra at the base of the spine. While She is living in the human body She is known as kundalini shakti, and presides over the totality of matter and energy that constitutes the entire phenomenal world. The goal of left-hand tantra is to attain Her grace and thereby experience Her manifestation in all forms of matter and energy. But under most circumstances kundalini shakti is asleep, and to gain access to Her abode and awaken Her the sages experimented with every possible means—including ingesting herbs, minerals, psychedelic drugs, and performing "forbidden" practices, as well as mantra, pranayama, and ritual. Ultimately they developed chakra puja, which they found to be the fastest way to pierce the chakras and experience oneness with Her.

Among other things chakra puja involves liquor, meat, fish, mudras (gestures), and physical union. It is called *vama marga*, "the left-hand path," as opposed to *dakshina marga*, "the right-hand path," in which these five components are prohibited. The left-hand path is controversial, and those who are not familiar with the scriptures and the oral tradition believe that it advocates drunkenness and orgies. This is a gross distortion. In fact there are stricter prerequisites to the left-hand path than the right-hand path, and following it requires more discipline, because the aspirant must maintain intense concentration on the practice in the midst of the strongest sensual stimulants. To make sure that the students walking this razor's edge keep their balance throughout, the practice is always done under the direct supervision of at least one adept (sometimes more), who monitors every step.

To stay tuned to the guru shakti (the shakti of the master) you replace your consciousness with his consciousness by means of intense contemplation, and throughout the chakra puja he is sitting in front of you. He carries you in his heart. He not only watches how you perform the rituals, hold your gestures, do your pranayama, or recite the mantras, he also observes your breathing patterns, which carry the signals of your subtle thoughts and feelings. Throughout the practice you maintain a meditative state in which you are aware of the presence of your master at the crown chakra and of the *ishta deva* (the personified form of the mantra) at the heart center. The moment your mind begins to waver, your master intercedes and brings it back to the *ishta deva*. Only because you are always so accompanied are you able to experience the oneness of mantra, deity, guru, and yantra in your own body. Your entire being becomes an eye. Regardless of what your physical eyes perceive, you see only what is within.

This inner awareness is the fruit of chakra puja, and to test its stability masters lead their students through many paradoxical experiences until they have attained perfect victory over the mind, senses, ego, and intellect. The goal, as illustrated by the following story, is to bring spirituality into day-to-day existence, and vice versa.

SHUKADEVA

In early childhood Shukadeva lost interest in worldly life and became a monk, committing himself to intense austerities and study of the scriptures. After years of sadhana he asked his father, the sage Vyasa, where and how he could find the highest wisdom, and Vyasa advised him to visit King Janaka, the wisest man and greatest yogi of that time.

When the young saint presented himself at the gate of Janaka's palace he was forced to wait a week before being admitted. Then he was ushered into a luxurious guest house in one of the palace gardens, where the atmosphere was in vivid contrast to anything he had encountered in his monkish existence—the rooms were richly furnished, beautiful women catered to his every wish—and the young ascetic felt as if he were suffocating. After several days in this oppressive atmosphere he was brought to the regal chambers, where he found the king lounging on a couch in his queen's embrace, a jeweled chalice in his hand. A maiden was soaking his left foot in hot water and his right foot was resting on the lap of another nubile young woman. Shukadeva found this incomprehensible.

King Janaka gestured casually for the young man to have a seat; the king seemed to be sunk in some sort of sensual stupor. But to Shukadeva's astonishment the king immediately turned the conversation to spiritual matters. He knew why the young man's father had sent him to the palace and even repeated the parting conversation that had taken place between father and son. In the midst of this two servants rushed into the room shouting that the east wing of the palace was in flames. Unperturbed, the king poured a few drops of water on his palms, closed his eyes for a moment, threw the water in the direction of the east wing, and resumed his conversation with Shukadeva. In a few minutes the servants returned with the news that the fire had been miraculously extinguished. King Janaka acknowledged the news without interrupting his conversation, and the young ascetic finally realized that the king was demonstrating complete mastery— fully established within himself, he was unaffected by liquor, women, and impending catastrophe.

CHAKRA PUJA

The goal of left-hand tantra is self-mastery, and to accomplish this end tantrics use liquor, meat, fish, mudras, and physical union in such a way that the wall between sense pleasure and divine ecstasy is demolished. Scriptures such as *Kularnava Tantra, Kamakhya Tantra,* and *Bagalamukhi Rahasyam* explain how the left-hand tantrics do the practices incorporating these "forbidden" ingredients. Prolonged mantra practice, the grace of the deity, and the blessings of the master enable them to induce the highest degree of spiritual awareness during the performance of chakra puja. But unless this awareness is cultivated, the act of eating and drinking is devoid of spiritual meaning.

The most important ingredient in the chakra puja ritual is liquor that has been derived from herbs and sanctified by the power of mantra and rituals. It must come from the master. Normally liquor contains energy that causes disorientation, inertia, and loss of memory, but by leading it through a multi-level spiritual processing (such as *shapa vimochana* and *amriti karana*) the master removes this energy and awakens spiritually illuminating properties in its place. Now this liquor is, figuratively speaking, liquid fire capable of consuming all impurities; only then is it ready to be used in the practice.

There is a specific way of receiving this drink from the master, pouring it into the chalice, and placing the chalice in the center of a special yantra drawn on the ground.

Next the aspirants perform a long ceremony consisting mainly of mantra recitation and mudras to propitiate the divinity that presides over the liquor. Then while sitting in the lotus posture or the accomplished pose, aspirants purify different aspects of their body, breath, senses, and mind by sprinkling liquor into their mouth as they perform *tattva mudra*. The mantras used during this purification are the same as those recited during *viraja homa*, the fire offering that accompanies the vows of renunciation. Next the aspirants invoke the sages of the lineage, Lord Ganesha (the remover of obstacles), and the presiding forces of the various chakras, and offer this sanctified liquor to them.

This is the initial part of the practice, and when it is completed the master permits the students to begin propitiating the kundalini shakti. This is done in five rounds of meditation

The yantra on which the chalice is placed

Tattva mudra

Tripada mudra (without and with chalice)

on Her, each beginning with a prolonged breathing practice, the recitation of prayers, mantra japa, and meditation. After the first round of meditation the student drinks a chalice of liquor. After the second round the aspirant takes a bite of meat and a second chalice of liquor. The third round entails a bite of fish and a third chalice of liquor, and the fourth, a bite of a dish made of deep-fried grains and a fourth chalice of liquor. After the fifth round of meditation the student mixes red and white sandalwood paste (a substitute for male and female sexual energy) and offers it to the kundalini shakti before drinking the final chalice of liquor.

Each round of meditation follows a similar pattern but some of the prayers are unique to a particular round. The first round of meditation on kundalini shakti is done in the following manner: before offering the liquor into the fire of kundalini the aspirants recite long prayers and do breathing practices that combine breath retention and mantra japa. While they sit with their head, neck, and trunk in a straight line and balance the chalice on a tripod formed by the thumb, index finger, and middle finger of their left hand, they meditate on the kundalini shakti that dwells in the muladhara center yet pervades the entire body. Through intense meditation they allow their individual consciousness to merge with the kundalini shakti, and while maintaining this state of oneness they take the chalice in their right hand and visualize the liquor being offered into the fire as they drink it.

The series of prayers (known as *patra vandana*, or chalice prayers) that precedes the offering of liquor in each round creates a contemplative mood and intensifies the practitioner's inner awareness. The chalice prayer recited during the first round of the offering, for example, invokes the three groups of sages of the lineage, Lord Ganesha, the three main centers of divinity within the body, and various groups of tantric adepts.

The chalice prayers also describe how liquor is a goddess at the esoteric level; when and how she was born; in what sense active and passive forms of bliss are associated with her; how the forces of creation, sustenance, and destruction emerged from the combination of the two aspects of bliss; and why liquor is the best offering that can be made to the fire of kundalini. In addition, by elucidating the symbolic meaning of the liquor, the chalice, and the rest of the ritual paraphernalia, these prayers help aspirants enliven their knowledge of tantric metaphysics with the spirit of love and surrender. The penultimate verse reminds the aspirants once again of who the masters are and reiterates that it is only with their permission that they are offering the nectar of liquor into the fire of kundalini shakti. Then they recite the final verse:

Ahanta patra bharitam idanta paramamritam.
Purnahanta maye vahnau juhomi shivarupa dhrik.

I, Shiva, offer the liquor of this-is-ness [objective awareness] contained in the chalice of I-am-ness [subjective awareness] into the fire of perfect I-am-ness [Supreme Consciousness].

While reciting these prayers aspirants are expected to visualize their body being replaced by the fire of kundalini, and while maintaining that awareness they drink the liquor until the chalice is empty. Subsequent rounds follow a similar pattern.

It is a myth that left-hand tantrics always use sex as a part of their practice. Actual physical union is involved only when aspirants have attained perfect mastery over their biochemistry as well as over their mind and senses. And only those who have attained perfect mastery of yoga techniques such as *khechari mudra, yoni mudra,* and *vajroli kriya* (and are thus able to force their sexual energy to travel upward) have the ability to incorporate physical union into the fifth round of chakra puja.

Drawing on the scriptures *Goraksha Samhita* and *Hatha Yoga Pradipika,* Mircea Eliade in his book *Yoga: Immortality and Freedom* explains chakra puja as follows: "To hasten the ascent of the kundalini, some tantric schools combined corporal positions *(mudra)* with sexual practices. The underlying idea was the necessity of achieving simultaneous 'immobility' of breath, thought, and semen. The *Goraksha Samhita* states that during the *khechari mudra* the bindu (= sperm) 'does not fall' even if one is embraced by a woman."

THE TRADITION

The tantric masters do not write about their sadhana or even talk about it to anyone other than initiates, and they require their students to take a vow never to disclose its exact method (although they are allowed to discuss the philosophy and metaphysics underlying these practices). This is why there is not a single scripture that contains complete information about how to purify the liquor and perform the chakra puja. However, for the sake of preserving a general knowledge of tantra as well as inspiring aspirants, adepts often write about practices into which they themselves have not been initiated, freely admitting that these manuals are incomplete and must be supplemented by the oral tradition. But they will never, under any circumstances, talk about the disciplines they themselves observe or the mantras they practice.

For example there is a scripture called *Prapanchasara,* attributed to the great master Shankaracharya with a commentary by his disciple Padma Pada. At one point the commentator explains the subtle differences among the twelve subtraditions of Sri Vidya. With one exception he offers an elaborate description of all these subtraditions, even giving mantras practiced by each. But when he comes to discuss the particular variation, *kadi vidya*, which is unique to his own tradition he simply says, "This great mantra is known to the whole world; there is no need to write about it."

Tantrics blanket themselves in seeming confusion, and in our search for tantric wisdom we must remember that what tantrics say is not necessarily what they do. Paradox and contradiction are hallmarks of the tradition, and to make sure that their students (as well as they themselves) are free from all temptation tantric masters perform rites that are incomprehensible to most of us. But underlying the contradictions, their social and moral behaviors are grounded in this simple formula: "Pig's droppings are as good as name, fame, and honor; being hailed as a guru is mere noise; ego is another form of drunkenness. Only after renouncing these three does one truly remember the name of God."

The left-hand school of kaula tantra is demanding and requires a great deal of preparation (and kaula tantra is only preliminary to the practices of the mishra and samaya schools). We need to be physically fit and emotionally balanced to undertake even the first level, the tantric practice of mantra sadhana. For example completing the purascharana that follows mantra initiation requires the freedom to organize our life around the practice. The second initiation and the practice following it is even more elaborate, and so requires even greater freedom. The first and most important requirement, therefore, is to gather our resources and minimize the obstacles to spiritual practices before undertaking them, and to this end tantric adepts discovered the techniques for awakening the forces of nature within and without so that the practitioner first becomes effective and successful in the world.

There are a number of tantric practices that have no direct bearing on spiritual enlightenment or experiencing oneness with the Divine; rather, their purpose is to help over-come specific problems, such as discord in the family, poverty, depression, grief, and anxiety. Tantrics see nothing wrong in using spiritual practices to draw a husband and wife closer together, for example. Their reasoning is that if a wife and husband understand each other they will not waste time and energy criticizing and quarreling; family life will be peaceful, and the time and energy saved can then be used for higher purposes. In addition there are practices for the welfare of humankind, for restoring harmony in nature, and for peace, to name a few.

Tantrics have also found that seeing a tangible result from a practice will help aspirants cultivate faith in tantric practices in general as well as remove obstacles that prevent them from undertaking higher practice; furthermore they can use this practice to help others overcome similar problems. For this reason the masters insist that if you wish to stay on the path and eventually achieve the highest goal of life you must do at least one of the tantric practices which shows an immediate result, even if the result is worldly. And therefore, to help you get started on the tantric path, we next describe a healing practice for calming phobia, nightmares, and disturbed sleep.

Chapter Seven

A PRACTICE FOR SEDUCING THE FORCES OF MATTER AND SPIRIT

*T*he practices that have made tantra popular are those that yield startling results quickly. They are simple and have few prerequisites. None of them has a direct effect on our spiritual growth; instead they help us achieve what we need to live a healthy and comfortable life. And if properly used they can help us remove obstacles that prevent us from engaging wholeheartedly in the spiritual quest.

The drawback is that after gaining the extraordinary powers induced by these practices students often become victims of their own achievement. For example a category of tantric practices known as *stambhana* gives the practitioner the capacity to immobilize. The energy it generates can be used either to immobilize our own negative tendencies or to immobilize another person's thinking or speaking capacity. How you use that energy is totally up to you, and it is easy to get excited and use it indiscriminately. That is why the scriptures advise that no matter how sincere you are or how accomplished, it is wise to study and practice under the supervision of a qualified teacher. Always have someone above you with the power and authority to point out your mistakes and help you correct them so that you stay on the right track.

There are thousands of relatively simple practices that yield startling results. They can be divided into eight categories:

1. Marana—practices to hurt, injure, or even kill

2. Mohana—practices to confuse and delude

3. Bashikarana—practices to subjugate, dominate, or manipulate

4. Ucchatana—practices to disrupt the flow of concentration and to create disinterestedness, frustration, and apathy

5. Vidveshana—practices to create hatred and animosity between people

6. Stambhana—practices to immobilize and render inert

7. Shanti karma—practices that lead to peace and happiness

8. Paushtika karma—practices that lead to health and healing

Practices in the first six categories can become a means to harm others, to feed our ego, to nurture our selfishness, and ultimately to block our spiritual growth; those in the last two categories are beneficial.

While I was visiting shrines and studying at the feet of the masters I learned several such practices that yield results quickly and have no harmful effect, either on the practitioner or on anyone else. They come from the most sublime tradition of tantra known as Sri Vidya, and they incorporate mantra, yantra, astrology, numerology, meditation, rituals, and a fire offering. These practices are done in several stages, and except for the step that gives the student the ability to transmit the power of the mantra to others, the student does not need to go through a formal process of initiation to undertake them. The only prerequisites are the basic meditation and pranayama practices, japa of the gayatri mantra, and the practice of non-violence, truthfulness, non-stealing, non-indulgence, non-possessiveness, cleanliness, contentment, self-discipline, self-reflection, and surrender to the Divine.

What follows are instructions for a healing practice of this nature for calming phobia, soothing disturbed sleep, and eradicating nightmares. For centuries people have used this and similar practices to achieve their desired goals, and both the scriptures and the oral tradition confirm their potency. If you choose to do the practice that follows, do not take it lightly just because it is simple and does not require much time. Do not modify the mantric injunctions or alter the perfectly balanced chemistry of the ritual ingredients. This practice is a meeting-ground of the spiritual dimensions of physics, chemistry, numerology, astrology, and mysticism, and completing the first three steps will yield a result that may well inspire you to begin your own tantric quest. Some of the ingredients may be difficult to find, but the more closely you can come to following the instructions exactly, the more powerful the result. And always remember: if you want to see a predictable result you must do this and other tantric practices at the right time and in the right place, and you must follow the ritual procedure precisely.

The Importance of Time and Place

Before describing the exact method of doing this practice let me explain the importance of time and place. Everything in nature is regulated by time. The life cycle follows the cycle of time called the seasons. The rotation of the seasons depends on the rotation of the earth on its axis and its movement around the sun. In the greater scheme the life of soil, water, plants, animals, humans, planets, stars, and constellations—everything—is governed by time. You will have a good harvest only if you plant on time—neither too early nor too late. Similarly you must know the right time to do this tantric practice if you wish to harvest the result.

For example the best time to begin your practice is on a Thursday, because in general the energy of the planet Jupiter has a greater positive influence on us on Thursday than on other days. If Thursday falls on the full moon or on the new moon or on the fifth and tenth days following either, the effect is even stronger. Tantrics call these *siddha yoga* times: when the astrological junctures are accompanied by forces conducive to success.

Further, any Thursday is best that falls on the full moon, or on the tenth day of the waxing fortnight, or on the fifth day of the waning fortnight. These timings can be further enhanced if the energy of specific constellations is also aligned with the planet earth. For example if on these days one of the constellations that have an auspicious influence on the earth is aligned with the earth, the practice will be even more fruitful. Such auspicious constellations for these kinds of practices are Rohini (Aldebaran), Ardra (Betelgeuse), Punarvasu (Pollux II), Pushya (delta Cancri), and Anuradha (delta Scorpio).

Place also plays an important role in the success and failure of any endeavor. For this particular practice the best place is a riverbank (of a river that is not polluted), a hilltop, a quiet area around a holy shrine, or an ashram where like-minded people are involved in similar practices. The more spiritually charged the place, the better it is. But if none of these is available then sit in your usual place for meditation and try to keep it as clean, uncluttered, and tranquil as possible.

Places often stricken by drought, fire, earthquakes, or hurricanes, or localities dominated by gangsters, drug dealers, and other criminals will invite obstacles and are to be avoided during this (and any) practice.

A PRACTICE FOR CALMING PHOBIA, NIGHTMARES, AND DISTURBED SLEEP

This is a healing practice. Its central focus is a yantra consisting of twenty-five squares and twenty-four tridents. The twenty-five squares represent the twenty-five elements: the five gross elements (earth, water, fire, air, and ether), the five subtle elements, the ten senses, mind, ego, intellect, prakriti (nature), and purusha (pure consciousness). Together these twenty-five elements encompass our entire existence as well as that of the cosmos.

The tridents represent the power of protection that comes from Shiva (pure consciousness). They are twenty-four in number, one for each square. The twenty-fifth square is the center of consciousness itself. And because consciousness is eternal, it requires no protection.

This particular practice is done in four separate steps. The numbers 1 through 5 that fill the squares in the first step of the practice refer to the five aspects of the primordial Divine Force, known respectively as Vama, Jyestha, Raudri, Shanta, and Ambika. Vama is the force of creativity; Jyestha, the force of maintenance; Raudri, destruction; Shanta, quietude; and Ambika, the power of Divine Will that inspires the four other forces to act. For the first two steps you need a board of mango wood or Himalayan cedar that is one-foot square, some fine powder of red sandalwood, and a nine-inch-long stick from a pomegranate tree, sharpened at one end.

Step One

How to Draw the Yantra

Assemble the ingredients next to your meditation seat, within easy reach. Spread a clean cloth (preferably red) in front of your seat (the cloth should be bigger than the board). Place the board on the cloth and take your seat.

Begin by putting about a half teaspoon of red sandalwood powder on the board. Spread it evenly with your fingers, and use more if needed. Draw the yantra with the sharpened stick. Draw the top line from left to right, starting from the upper left-hand corner. Then draw the vertical line on the side of the left edge from top to bottom. Next draw the bottom line from left to right, followed by the vertical line on the side of the right edge from top to bottom. Then draw the four remaining horizontal lines from top to bottom, moving from left to right. Finally add the four remaining vertical lines, beginning with the line at the left, drawing them from top to bottom. You now have twenty-five squares. Draw twenty-four tridents outside the grand square by extending each line.

Fill the squares with numbers 1 through 5, as shown below. Start with the top row and fill in the squares according to the following numerical sequence: in the top row fill the first square with "1," then the fourth square with "2," then the second square with "3," then the fifth square with "4," and finally the third square with "5." Follow the same procedure for the squares in the remaining four lines. Take care to keep the board level and steady so that the powder does not shift and blur the yantra.

1	3	5	2	4
5	2	4	1	3
4	1	3	5	2
3	5	2	4	1
2	4	3	1	5

Yantra for Step One

How to Meditate on the Yantra

When you have completed the yantra hold your hands to your heart in trikhanda mudra and meditate on the yantra or its corresponding deity. Or if you have found and developed an affinity with the personified form of your mantra, you meditate on that. If you cannot do either of these, simply meditate on the flame in the cave of your heart while repeating the gayatri mantra once.

Then take a deep breath, bring your hands (still in trikhanda mudra) to your nostrils, and exhale into the palms of your hands. During the exhalation visualize the deity in the form of divine light traveling from your heart and entering the hollow of the mudra. Maintaining awareness that the Divinity is contained in the mudra, bring your hands to the yantra and release the mudra, letting the energy flow onto the yantra.

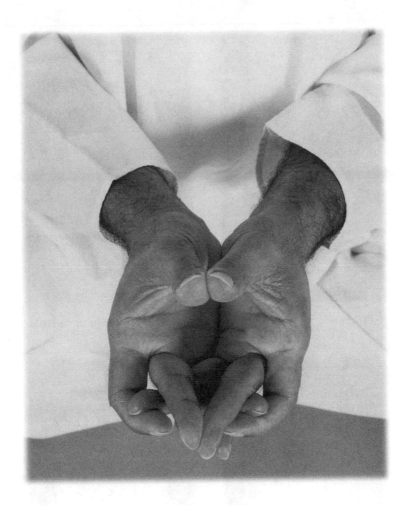

Trikhanda mudra

Trikhanda mudra at heart

Trikhanda mudra at nostrils

Trikhanda mudra to yantra

*Trikhanda mudra
released to yantra*

To reinforce the presence of the deity in the yantra, recite the *prana pratistha* mantra (the mantra for imbuing the yantra with the power of the deity):

Om am hrim krom yam ram lam vam sham sham sam ham hamsah so ham mama asmin yantre mama ishta devah ihaiva-gatya sukham chiram tishthatu svaha. Om om om pratistha.

Then worship the yantra mentally by making the following offerings to the Divinity that now resides in the yantra:

Lam   (I offer the earth element as fragrant paste).

Ham   (I offer ether as flowers and garlands).

Yam   (I offer the air element as incense).

Ram   (I offer the fire element as a lamp).

Vam   (I offer the water element as food and drink).

Sam   (I surrender myself to the Divinity residing in this yantra).

Then do twelve hundred repetitions of the gayatri mantra (twelve rounds on a mala), and at the end of the japa (repetition of the mantra) bring your hands to the yantra in *samhara mudra*. With intense contemplation feel the energy of the yantra entering the mudra. Bring your hands to your nostrils and inhale deeply. During the inhalation feel the energy of the deity traveling through your nostrils and coming to rest in your heart, as you bring the mudra to your heart. Release the mudra and press your palms together at your heart.

Now erase the yantra. Shake the powder onto a sheet of paper and collect it in a bottle to be used again the next day. Continue this practice for forty days.

This level of the practice benefits only the practitioner: in other words you cannot transmit the energy it generates to someone else to solve his or her problems. When you have completed the practice you can either take a break of a few days or weeks or begin the next step the next day.

Samhara mudra

Step Two

Step two is more potent than step one, and completing step one is its prerequisite. Only those who have been formally initiated into Sri Vidya practice can undertake this step without having completed the first.

Draw the yantra precisely as you did during the first step of the practice. The only difference is that now the numbers are replaced by the letters of a special mantra, *Namah Shivaya*, written in Devanagari (the script in which Sanskrit is written). Tantrics believe that every letter in the Devanagari script is a yantra in itself, and therefore in the practice of a yantra the Sanskrit letters of the mantra cannot be replaced with another script. In Devanagari script this mantra consists of five letters, and that is why it is called *panchakshara* (the

$$ॐ \; नमः \; शिवाय$$

five-syllable mantra). The placement of the letters follow the same sequence as the placement of the numbers in the yantra in step one.

After drawing the yantra and filling the squares with the letters of the mantra, follow the same procedure you followed in step one: perform trikhanda mudra, recite the prana pratistha mantra, perform the mental worship, do twelve rounds of japa of the gayatri mantra, and when you are finished, draw the energy back with samhara mudra. Continue this practice for forty days.

This step is more powerful than the first, but like step one, this level of practice is intended to benefit only the practitioner—the energy cannot be transmitted to benefit others.

न	शि	य	मः	वा
य	मः	वा	न	शि
वा	न	शि	य	मः
शि	य	मः	वा	न
मः	वा	न	शि	य

Yantra for Step Two

Samhara mudra at yantra

Samhara mudra at nostrils

Samhara mudra at heart

Palms together at heart

Step Three

This third step is more potent still, and again steps one and two are prerequisites for anyone who has not been formally initiated into the practice of Sri Vidya.

The yantra is the same as the one you drew in step two, only this time it is drawn on the palm of the left hand, using the ring finger of the right hand as the pen and pure water from a copper or silver vessel as ink. Obviously the space on your left palm is not big enough to draw the entire yantra legibly. Inscribing it on the palm is simply a device for inscribing the yantra on the screen of your mind.

In this step there is no need to invite the deity in your heart to reside in the yantra—there is no need to recite the prana pratistha mantra or at the conclusion of the japa to draw the energy back into your heart with samhara mudra. Simply do the mental worship before you begin japa of the gayatri mantra. As in step two, you do twelve hundred repetitions of the gayatri mantra each day for forty days. Again, the energy generated by this practice cannot be transmitted to others.

Step Four

Only those who have received formal initiation into the practice of Sri Vidya are entitled to undertake the fourth step of this practice. Unlike the first three steps, which can be done by following the instructions just given, this step can be practiced only if it is received directly from a master. After you have completed it you are fully capable of transmitting the healing energy of the practice to anyone, and you are authorized to do so.

The method of healing others with the power of the practice is simple: you can draw the yantra corresponding to the yantra in step two on a piece of birch bark, breathe life into it, and give it to someone in need. It will work instantly, even if the person receiving it has no capacity to do any practice, no interest in such practices, no faith in this practice, and even no respect for it. The person who has mastered this final stage can also help others from a distance even without localizing the energy in a yantra. Such a one is like a living yantra and can transmit the healing energy by means of thought, sight, speech, and touch. The blessings of practitioners of this caliber have the capacity to heal others —the healing energy emits from them at will and yet is never exhausted.

Here is how this step is done. You have already been initiated into Sri Vidya, and you know the elaborate and multi-level practices of nyasas for synchronizing the forces of Sri Chakra with the forces in your body. You know how to meditate on the personified form of Sri Vidya or on Her yantric form, Sri Chakra. As you begin this specific practice you replace yourself with the personified form of Sri Vidya through intense visualization. Your concentration is such that you no longer exist—She alone exists. Therefore it is She who is doing the practice. You may meditate on the yantra as

Sri Vidya

described in step two—in pure light or in the heart center (but remember that the heart center is no longer your heart center).

As far as japa is concerned, now the gayatri mantra is replaced by the twenty-fourth mantra of *Saundaryalahari* (*The Wave of Beauty and Bliss*), the most revered scripture in the tradition of Sri Vidya:

जगत्सूते धाता हरिरवति रुद्रः क्षपयते
तिरस्कुर्वन्नेतत् स्वमपि वपुर शस्तिरयति ।
सदा पूर्वः सर्वं तदिदमनुगृह्णाति च शिवः
तवाज्ञामालम्ब्य क्षणचलितयोर्भ्रूलतिकयोः ॥

Jagat suta dhata hariravati rudrah kshapayate
tiraskurvan etat svamapi vapurishas tirayati;
sada-purvah sarvam tad idam anugrihnati cha Shivah
tavajnam alambya kshna-chalitayor bhru-latikayoh.

Obeying the command issuing from the movement of
　　your eyebrows,
Brahma creates the universe. Vishnu sustains it.
Shiva destroys it. Ishvara conceals it.
And Sadashiva inspires all the forces to act.

According to the commentators on this scripture you are supposed to recite this mantra a thousand times a day for forty days. However, the oral tradition insists that if you have been initiated into Sri Vidya then thirty-three repetitions is sufficient, and you need to do it for only thirty-three days.

The final event in this practice is the fire offering, which is done at the end of thirty-three days. The first offering must be done in a precise manner. How you construct the fire pit, what kind of sticks you use for making the fire, the source of the fire, and the invocation of the specific forces to whom the offerings are made are crucial to the practice. If you do not know how to do these things seek help from someone who does. (Ordinarily these fire rituals are done by a group of aspirants, at least one of whom knows the basic mantras and the procedure for making the fire.) Time and place are also crucial. Everything must be clean: the bricks used to construct the fire pit, the sticks to be burned, the ingredients to be offered, and the utensils used during the offering.

The fire pit should be below ground level so that you are not exposed to the fire directly; its size and shape depend on the size and the goal of the offering. In this case, a square fire pit is the best. It is surrounded by three concentric borders, which symbolize the physical, subtle, and casual bodies; the power of will, the power of knowledge, and the power of action; the three states of consciousness (waking, dreaming, and deep sleep); and the forces of creation, maintenance, and destruction.

Once the fire pit is ready, arrange all the objects to be used in the fire offering in proper sequence and place them within your reach so you do not have to get up when you need them. Then prepare to light the fire. This includes invoking the guru shakti of the lineage, your ishta deva, and (most importantly) Lord Ganesha, who removes all obstacles. During the invocation of Ganesha you remind yourself of how He helps attain freedom from fear, insecurity, anger, sensuality, grief, sloth, inertia, and frustration.

Then you invoke and receive the blessings of the forces— ten in number—that protect and guide all ten directions, all roads and paths. These forces help our ten senses to function in a healthy and joyful manner. Then you invoke the energies of the ten planets, which influence every aspect of our life.

After this basic invocation tantrics recite a group of mantras known as *Vishvedeva Sukta*, which is dedicated to all the divine forces which rule over mind, matter, and energy within and without, both at the individual and cosmic level. Then, once you have offered the rightful place to all the forces of nature, both in your heart and next to the fire pit, you ignite the fire. This is also done with the aid of mantra (and again, if you do not know the mantras for igniting the fire you must seek help from someone who does).

The source of the fire affects the success of your practice. Fire brought from the fire pit of an accomplished master is the best. If that is not available then the fire should be ignited by the hands of someone whose kundalini shakti is awakened. If such a person is not available then use matches and ignite the fire while reciting the fire mantras from the *Rig Veda* and the *Yajur Veda*. The power of the fire mantra will compensate for all missing ingredients.

Once the fire is lit a minimum of nine offerings of ghee (clarified butter) are made to the fire itself while reciting the first nine mantras of the *Rig Veda*. You begin the main course of the fire practice only after you have made these initial offerings. Now the offerings consist of black sesame seeds, raw sugar from sugarcane juice, more ghee, and herbs—mainly apamarga (*Acyranthus aspera*), brahmi (*Bacopa monniera*), guggula (*Commiphora mukul*), and the flowers of red hibiscus

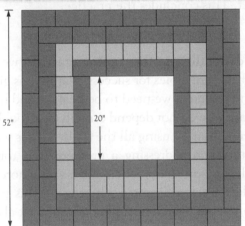

Fire Pit

(*Hibiscus rosa-sinensis*), aparajita (*Clitonia ternatea*), and kaner (*Nerium indicum*). First you make one offering each to the guru shakti of the lineage, to Ganesha, to your ishta deva, to the protectors of the ten directions, and to the nine planets.

Then you make 108 offerings while repeating the special mantra from *Saundaryalahari* which you used for your japa. Before each offering you repeat the mantra, adding the word *svaha* at the end as you put it into the fire. After the 108 offerings you surrender the fruit of your entire practice to the fire. Then you bring your hands in trikhanda mudra to the fire pit, visualize the power of the fire entering the mudra, and bring the mudra to your nostrils; inhale, and visualize the power of the fire traveling from your nostrils and coming to rest in your heart center. This concludes the practice.

A BALANCED APPROACH

While doing this or other tantric practices we must not ignore the basic principles for success. Nature has given us all the tools and resources we need to be healthy and happy, and those who are wise do not depend on only one tool but rather create a mechanism for using all the tools. This is what tantra is all about. When addressing a problem it is totally non-tantric to depend on the practice alone and ignore all other possible solutions. For example when using this practice to calm the mind and overcome a phobia you must also include the standard treatment that includes psychotherapy, medication, exercise, and dietary principles. Tantrics tell the following story to illustrate the importance of a balanced approach to solving problems.

There was a learned pandit who wanted to have a long life, free from sickness and old age, so that he could commit himself wholeheartedly to his spiritual practices. Intent on health and longevity, he began a rigorous practice. He built his hut on the bank of a river and undertook a purascharana of a mantra, a practice so intense that it consumed most of his days and nights, and little time was left for resting and eating. He quickly became haggard and weak, prey to coughs, colds, and a host of other illnesses. Still he dragged himself through the practice, consoling himself at times with the thought that his health problems were obstacles he must confront and conquer. At other times he told himself that the purifying effect of the mantra was bringing up these ailments and soon his body and mind would be so cleansed that illness would never visit him again.

One hot summer day he came out of his hut and was astonished to see a young man grinding dry sand in a stone pit nearby. He had yoked a pair of bulls to a grinding rod, and they were walking around and around the pit, causing the rod to press the sand. When the pandit asked why, the young man replied, "I am pressing this sand because I need milk."

"Have you lost your mind?" the pandit exclaimed. "How can you get milk from sand? Milk comes from a cow."

"Nothing is impossible if you are fully determined and your intentions are good. If someone can achieve health and longevity by doing spiritual practice while ignoring the most basic principles of health, why can't I get milk out of sand?"

Instantly realizing that this young man was the materialized form of mantra shakti the pandit fell at his feet, and the young man appeared in the form of Indra, the presiding force of the cosmic mind. Indra then instructed the pandit in the higher practices of hatha and kundalini yoga and taught him how to do his purascharana in such a way that all obstacles would be removed and the fountain of youth spring forth and nourish his vitality and sustain his body and mind. This story comes from the yogis of Guru Gorakhnatha's tradition, and they tell us that this pandit later came to be known as

Prabhudeva, whose name appears in the *Hatha Yoga Pradipika* among the *siddha* masters who have conquered death.

Tantric practices are potent: they are designed to seduce the forces of nature to bring about extraordinary changes in both the material and spiritual realms. For example the concentrated energy of sound (mantra) and form (yantra) can be used to polarize the energy released from the herbs used in the fire offering and (further guided by the power of the mind) to stir the subtle properties of matter, mind, and consciousness at will. The secret of tantric "miracles" lies in gaining access to the subtle forces of nature, learning to understand their dynamics, and acquiring the ability to use them to override the normal pattern of events. Whether we do this to enhance spiritual progress or achieve trivial, worldly goals is totally up to us.

GLOSSARY

AMRITI KARANA • *A tantric procedure consisting of mantra recitation and performance of mudra to divinize ritual objects with the energy of elixir.*

ANANDA VANA • *"Forest of bliss." Another name for Banaras.*

APARAJITA VIDYA • *"Knowledge pertaining to the Invincible One." Another name for Sri Vidya or the goddess Durga.*

AUGHAR • *"Non-terrible." One of the more esoteric of the tantric traditions; also known as aghora.*

AVIGHNESHA • *The lord who brings success without obstacles; the remover of obstacles; the lord Ganesha.*

BAGALAMUKHI • *An esoteric tantric path belonging to one of the ten great goddesses; the queen of forbidden tantra; synonymous with Brahmastra, the highest weapon of Brahman.*

BASHIKARANA • *Tantric practices to subjugate and dominate others.*

BHAIRAVA • *The most vibrant form of Shiva; often associated with destruction; the form of Shiva that destroys our ignorance and grants mental clarity and spiritual illumination.*

BHOGA • *Worldly pleasure; enjoyment.*

BHUMI SAMADHI • *The practice of voluntarily casting off the body underground.*

BINDU • *"Dot; drop." Technical tantric term for liquor; in alchemy: the metal mercury, or sexual energy; in kundalini yoga: the concentrated energy field at or above the ajña chakra (the eyebrow center).*

BRAHMACHARYA • *Practice leading to the realization of Brahman; often used synonymously with celibacy.*

BRAHMA NADI • *The energy channel that flows between the eyebrow center and the sahasrara chakra (the center at the crown of the head).*

BRAHMASTRA • *"The weapon of Brahman." The force engendered by tantric practices to destroy the ultimate enemy, ignorance; the tantric name for the goddess Bagalamukhi.*

CHAKRA • *"Wheel." A center of consciousness within the body corresponding to a major nerve plexus of the gross physical nervous system situated along the spinal cord; a circle formed around the master for left-hand tantric rituals; synonymous with yantra and mandala.*

CHAKRA PUJA • *"Worshipping the chakras." A special term referring to the left-hand tantric practice that employs liquor, meat, fish, mudras, and physical union or its substitute; the tantric practice which is done by a group of practitioners under the supervision of a master.*

CHAKRESHVARA • *The lord of the chakras; the presiding deity of a chakra in the human body; the master, the lord of the circle in chakra puja.*

CHANDRA VIJÑANA • *"The lunar science." The mystical knowledge of the moon; another term for Sri Vidya.*

CHHINNAMASTA • *An esoteric tantric path belonging to one of the ten great goddesses; the representative of the energy of transcendental consciousness.*

CHYME • *Digested food in liquid form, right before it is absorbed into the bloodstream; first among the seven constituents of the human body.*

DAKSHINA MARGA • *The right-hand path of kaula tantra.*

DARSHANA • *"Glimpse." The direct vision of the invisible, absolute reality; revelation; system of philosophy.*

DATTATREYA • *A prominent sage believed to be immortal and still guiding aspirants; the son of sage Atri and Anasuya; the sage referred to as the seer of several mantras in both Vedic and tantric scriptures.*

GORAKHNATHA • *A siddha master who attained immortality through the practice of hatha yoga and alchemy; an immortal yogi honored in Tibetan, Nepalese, and Indian traditions.*

HATHA YOGA • *The school that aims to balance solar and lunar and masculine and feminine energies by means of postures, breathing techniques, cleansing practices, mudras, and meditation.*

HRIDAYA • *"Heart." The tantric term referring to the aspect of mantra which is to be visualized at the heart center or to be synchronized with the energy of the heart center; a practice consisting of a recitation of a long set of mantras that enables the practitioner to induce a state of oneness between the power of mantra and oneself.*

ISHTA DEVA • *A personal form of the Impersonal Divine Being; a personified form of a mantra.*

ISHVARA • *The Almighty Divine Being; the divine force endowed with the unrestricted power of will.*

JAPA • *Repetition of a mantra.*

JIVA • *Individual self; the soul, the innermost aspect of ourselves; in the samaya school of tantra: the final constituent of our existence.*

KALA BHAIRAVA • *The most vibrant form of Shiva; often referred to as the Lord of Time; the Divine Force through whose grace a series of events manifest in the realm of time.*

KALA CHAKRA • *The wheel of time; famous Buddhist yantra.*

KALI • *Consort of Shiva; one of the ten maha vidyas; the ruler of time, often associated with Kala Bhairava or Mahakala.*

KASHI • *"City of Light." Another name for Banaras.*

KAULA • *"That which is related to family." The tantric school characterized by external practices; includes both right- and left-hand paths.*

KAVACHA • *"Armor." The portion of mantra that corresponds to the energies of the front, back, left, and right sides of the body and thus, like armor, protects the aspirant from obstacles.*

KILAKA • *"Anchor." The portion of the mantra that serves as an anchor to all other aspects of the mantra; a seed mantra that stabilizes the mind and unites it with the power of the mantra.*

KUNDALINI SHAKTI • *The primordial divine force; the dormant energy that yogis awaken through yogic means; in the latent form it resides in the muladhara chakra.*

KUNDALINI YOGA • *A system of practice that includes the use of mantras, yantras, mudras, and breathing exercises to awaken the latent kundalini in the muladhara chakra and channel it upward to the highest chakra, the sahasrara.*

LAKSHAMANA REKHA • *Protective line used in tantric rites.*

LAKSHMI • *The goddess of wealth and prosperity; the power of nurturance; consort of Lord Vishnu.*

MAHAKALA • *The devourer of time; the presiding deity of all the shrines in Ujjain; also known as the destroyer of death.*

MAHA MRITYUNJAYA • *"The great conqueror of death." The form of Shiva that grants immortality and freedom from all pains and miseries; the famous healing mantra first mentioned in the Yajur Veda and further elaborated in tantric scriptures.*

MAHA VIDYA • *"Great knowledge." The ten manifestations of the Divine Mother: Kali, Tara, Chhinnamasta, Tripura (Sri Vidya), Tripura Bhairavi, Bagalamukhi, Bhuvaneshvari, Matangi, Kamala, and Dhumavati.*

MANGALANATHA • *The presiding deity of the planet Mars.*

MANIPURA CHAKRA • *"Chakra of shining gems." The navel center; the solar plexus; center governing the energy of fire.*

MARANA • *A tantric practice for hurting or killing; a low-grade practice belonging to black magic.*

MATANGI • *One of the ten maha vidyas; in tantric texts, also known as Shyamala and Shuka Shyamala; the goddess often associated with Sarasvati, the goddess of wisdom and fine arts; the shrine associated with her near Chitrakut is known as Maihar.*

MATHA • Monastery; center of learning.

MISHRA • "Mixture, combination." The school of tantra combining external rituals and meditative techniques.

MOHANA • A tantric practice to influence the minds of others.

MOKSHA • Liberation; freedom from the bondage of karma and the cycle of birth and death.

MUDRA • "Seal." Any of a number of specific hand gestures used during yogic and tantric rituals.

MULADHARA CHAKRA • The first chakra, corresponding to the nerve plexus at the base of the spine.

NADA YOGA • The school of yoga in which the practitioners meditate on the eternal sound.

NAVA RATRI • "Nine nights." Nine specific days dedicated to the worship of the Divine Mother; they fall roughly during March/April and again September/October.

NYASA • A technique for synchronizing different aspects of a mantra with different parts of the human body.

OJAS • The finest form of the life-force; the source of vigor and vitality.

PALI • The language of the Buddhist scriptures.

PANCHAKSHARA • *The five-syllable mantra Namah Shivaya.*

PARAKAYA PRAVESHA • *The yogic technique of leaving the body without dying and entering another body without being born; this usually refers to the process of entering a fresh corpse, thus bringing it back to life.*

PATALA • *"Flower petals." A practice consisting of the recitation of a long set of mantras and prayers.*

PATRA VANDANA • *The special prayer recited during chakra puja; through this prayer tantrics invoke the Divine Force in the chalice and divinize the entire process of grasping the chalice, extending it to the master, receiving liquor in it, and holding it in tripada mudra before drinking the sanctified liquid.*

PAUSHTIKA KARMA • *Tantric practices for health and healing.*

PITHA SHAKTI • *The forces that constitute the base of the shrine; the forces which serve as a seat for the main deity or the mantra shakti; the forces that help an aspirant to remain firm and stable throughout all storms and commotions during the practice.*

PRAKRITA • *The language of the Jaina scriptures.*

PRANA PRATISTHA • *"Establishment of prana." Invoking the deity and imbuing one's heart with that energy before starting the main course of japa or meditation on that deity; it is done by reciting mantras from either Vedic or tantric sources, or from both, and further combining it with visualization of the deity or the light at the heart center.*

PRANAYAMA • *"Expansion of prana, the life-force." Breathing techniques leading to the mastery over the pranic force; the science of prana that enables an aspirant to gain access to the pranamaya kosha, the pranic body that lies beyond the physical body.*

PRAYOGA SHASTRA • *Scriptures setting forth advanced yogic and tantric practices and their application.*

PURASCHARANA • *"Taking the first step." The practice of completing a specific amount of mantra japa in a specific period of time while observing a specific set of disciplines.*

SAHASRARA CHAKRA • *"Thousand-petaled chakra." The highest chakra, located at the crown center.*

SAMAYA • *"One with Her." The purely meditative school of tantra in which all practices are done while maintaining an awareness of oneness with the Divine within.*

SANDHYOPASANA • *"Twilight meditation." A set of auxiliary practices done before japa of the gayatri mantra.*

SARASVATI • *The goddess of the ever-flowing stream of creativity; the goddess of wisdom and fine arts.*

SHAKTIPATA • *The direct transmission of spiritual energy; the process and event of spiritual energy being transmitted from guru to disciple.*

SHANTI KARMA • *"Peaceful practices." Tantric practices leading to peace and happiness.*

SHAPA VIMOCHANA • *A tantric practice for removing the conditions that prevent a practitioner from attaining success in the practice of tantric mantras.*

SHIVA BALI • *Dedicating or surrendering oneself to Shiva, the primordial force of creativity; offering of food, in most cases a non-vegetarian dish, to jackals.*

SIDDHA YOGA • *The alignment of constellations and planets which, by their inherent virtue, have a positive influence on the spiritual forces on the planet earth; astrological junctures accompanied by forces conducive to success.*

SIDDHI • *Spiritual power; the power of success; extraordinary ability; supernatural power gained through tantric practices; psychic power.*

SRI CHAKRA • *The chakra of the Divine Mother, Sri; the chakra of supreme beauty and bliss; the chakra of the Most Auspicious One; the geometrical form of Sri Vidya; the highest yantra, which according to tantrics is a complete map of the microcosm and the macrocosm.*

SRI MATA • *The Divine Mother, Sri Vidya; the ultimate divine force.*

SRI VIDYA • *"Auspicious wisdom." The most complete and comprehensive of the ten maha vidyas; the presiding deity of Sri Chakra.*

SRI YANTRA • *Another name of Sri Chakra.*

STAMBHANA • *Tantric practices to immobilize or render inert.*

SURYA VIJÑANA • *"The science of the sun." The solar sciences; the mystical knowledge of the sun; the practices pertaining to the navel center.*

TAPAS • *"That which generates heat." Spiritual discipline; austerity; the practices for taming the senses and mind.*

TARA • *"The force that helps us cross the ocean of pain and misery"; "star." One of the ten maha vidyas.*

TIRTHA RAJA • *"Lord of shrines." Also known as Prayaga Raja; another name for Allahabad.*

TRIPURA SUNDARI • *"The most beautiful goddess in the triple world." Another name for Sri Vidya.*

UCCHATANA • *Disrupting the flow of concentration and engendering uninterest, frustration, and apathy; a set of tantric practices to create disturbance in the minds of others.*

UPASANA • *"Sitting near." Worship; tantric practices consisting of rituals, recitation of prayers, and other external practices which help an aspirant draw closer to the Divine.*

VAIRAGI • *One who is not attracted by the charms and temptations of the world; a person practicing non-attachment and dispassion.*

VAMA MARGA • *The left-hand path of kaula tantra, characterized by the use of liquor, meat, fish, mudras, and symbolic or actual physical union.*

VASHIKARANA • *The process of subduing or dominating others; a set of tantric practices for seduction.*

VEDANTA • *"The end or culmination of the Vedas." The highest form of Vedic wisdom; the Upanishads; a school of Indian philosophy.*

VIDVESHANA • *The process of creating animosity and hatred; tantric practices for creating animosity between two people.*

VIGHNAKARTA • *The creator of obstacles; Lord Ganesha, who is also the remover of obstacles.*

VIKRANTA BHAIRAVA • *The most transcendent form of Bhairava; a special shrine on the outskirts of Ujjain.*

VIRAJA HOMA • *"The dustless fire offering." The fire offering that consumes all impurities; the fire offering that accompanies the vows of renunciation.*

VYAHRITI • *"Covering." The first words (bhur bhuvah svah) added at the beginning of the gayatri mantra.*

YANTRA • *"Device." A geometric representation of mantric energy; the Divine Force in the form of light.*

About the Author

PANDIT RAJMANI TIGUNAIT, PHD, is a modern-day master and living link in the unbroken Himalayan Tradition. He embodies the yogic and tantric wisdom which the Himalayan Tradition has safeguarded for thousands of years. Pandit Tigunait is the successor of Sri Swami Rama of the Himalayas and the spiritual head of the Himalayan Institute. As a young man he committed himself to arduous spiritual practice and studied with renowned adepts of India before being initiated into the lineage of the Himalayan Tradition by his master, Sri Swami Rama, in 1976.

Pandit Tigunait is fluent in Vedic and Classical Sanskrit and holds two doctorates, one from the University of Allahabad (India), and another from the University of Pennsylvania. As a leading voice of YogaInternational.com and the author of 15 books, his teachings span a wide range, from scholarly analysis and scripture translation to practical guidance on applying yogic wisdom to modern life. Over the past 35 years, Pandit Tigunait has touched innumerable lives around the world as a teacher, guide, author, humanitarian, and visionary spiritual leader.

The main building of the Himalayan Institute headquarters near Honesdale, Pennsylvania

The Himalayan Institute

A leader in the field of yoga, meditation, spirituality, and holistic health, the Himalayan Institute is a nonprofit international organization dedicated to serving humanity through educational, spiritual, and humanitarian programs. The mission of the Himalayan Institute is to inspire, educate, and empower all those who seek to experience their full potential.

Founded in 1971 by Swami Rama of the Himalayas, the Himalayan Institute and its varied activities and programs exemplify the spiritual heritage of mankind that unites East and West, spirituality and science, ancient wisdom and modern technology.

Our international headquarters is located on a beautiful 400-acre campus in the rolling hills of the Pocono Mountains of northeastern Pennsylvania. Our spiritually vibrant community and peaceful setting provide the perfect atmosphere for seminars and retreats, residential programs, and holistic health services. Students from all over the world join us to attend diverse programs on subjects such as hatha yoga, meditation, stress reduction, ayurveda, and yoga and tantra philosophy.

In addition, the Himalayan Institute draws on roots in the yoga tradition to serve our members and community through the following programs, services, and products:

Mission Programs
The essence of the Himalayan Institute's teaching mission flows from the timeless message of the Himalayan Masters, and is echoed in our on-site mission programming. Their message is to first become aware of the reality within ourselves, and then to build a bridge between our inner and outer worlds.

Our mission programs express a rich body of experiential wisdom and are offered year-round. They include seminars, retreats, and professional certifications that bring you the best of an authentic yoga tradition, addressed to a modern audience. Join us on campus for our Mission Programs to find wisdom from the heart of the yoga tradition, guidance for authentic practice, and food for your soul.

Wisdom Library and Mission Membership
The Himalayan Institute online Wisdom Library curates the essential teachings of the living Himalayan Tradition. This offering is a unique counterpart to our in-person Mission Programs, empowering students by providing online learning resources to enrich their study and practice outside the classroom.

Our Wisdom Library features multimedia blog content, livestreams, podcasts, downloadable practice resources, digital courses, and an interactive Seeker's Forum. These teachings capture our Mission Faculty's decades of study, practice, and teaching experience, featuring new content as well as the timeless teachings of Swami Rama and Pandit Rajmani Tigunait.

We invite seekers and students of the Himalayan Tradition to become a Himalayan Institute Mission Member, which grants unlimited access to the Wisdom Library. Mission Membership offers a way for you to support our shared commitment to service, while deepening your study and practice in the living Himalayan Tradition.

Spiritual Excursions
Since 1972, the Himalayan Institute has been organizing pilgrimages for spiritual seekers from around the world. Our spiritual excursions follow the traditional pilgrimage routes where adepts of the Himalayas lived and practiced. For thousands of years, pilgrimage has been an essential part of yoga sadhana, offering spiritual seekers the opportunity to experience the transformative power of living shrines of the Himalayan Tradition.

Global Humanitarian Projects

The Himalayan Institute's humanitarian mission is yoga in action—offering spiritually grounded healing and transformation to the world. Our humanitarian projects serve impoverished communities in India, Mexico, and Cameroon through rural empowerment and environmental regeneration. By putting yoga philosophy into practice, our programs are empowering communities globally with the knowledge and tools needed for a lasting social transformation at the grassroots level.

Publications

The Himalayan Institute publishes over 60 titles on yoga, philosophy, spirituality, science, ayurveda, and holistic health. These include the best-selling books *Living with the Himalayan Masters* and *The Science of Breath*, by Swami Rama; *The Power of Mantra and the Mystery of Initiation, From Death to Birth, Tantra Unveiled,* and two commentaries on the *Yoga Sutra—The Secret of the Yoga Sutra: Samadhi Pada* and *The Practice of the Yoga Sutra: Sadhana Pada*— by Pandit Rajmani Tigunait, PhD; and the award-winning *Yoga: Mastering the Basics* by Sandra Anderson and Rolf Sovik, PsyD. These books are for everyone: the interested reader, the spiritual novice, and the experienced practitioner.

PureRejuv Wellness Center

For over 40 years, the PureRejuv Wellness Center has fulfilled part of the Institute's mission to promote healthy and sustainable lifestyles. PureRejuv combines Eastern philosophy and Western medicine in an integrated approach to holistic health—nurturing balance and healing at home and at work. We offer the opportunity to find healing and renewal through on-site wellness retreats and individual wellness services, including therapeutic massage and bodywork, yoga therapy, ayurveda, biofeedback, natural medicine, and one-on-one consultations with our integrative medical staff.

Total Health Products

The Himalayan Institute, the developer of the original Neti Pot, manufactures a health line specializing in traditional and modern ayurvedic supplements and body care. We are dedicated to holistic and natural living by providing products using non-GMO components, petroleum-free biodegrading plastics, and eco-friendly packaging that has the least impact on the environment. Part of every purchase supports our Global Humanitarian projects, further developing and reinforcing our core mission of spirituality in action.

For further information about our programs, humanitarian projects, and products:

call: 800.822.4547
e-mail: info@HimalayanInstitute.org
write: The Himalayan Institute
          952 Bethany Turnpike
          Honesdale, PA 18431
or visit: HimalayanInstitute.org

HIMALAYAN INSTITUTE®

inherit the wisdom of a living tradition today!

As a Mission Member, you will gain exclusive access to our online Wisdom Library. The Wisdom Library includes monthly livestream workshops, digital practicums and eCourses, monthly podcasts with Himalayan Institute Mission Faculty, and multimedia practice resources.

Wisdom Library

Netra Tantra: Harnessing the Healing Force (Part 1)
Pandit Rajmani Tigunait, PhD | September 29, 2017
Read more

• • •

Mission Membership Benefits

- **Never-before-seen content from Swami Rama & Pandit Tigunait**
- **New content announcements & weekly blog roundup**
- **Unlimited access to online yoga classes and meditation classes**
- **Members only digital workshops and monthly livestreams**
- **Downloadable practice resources and Prayers of the Tradition**

Get FREE access to the Wisdom Library for 30 days!

Mission Membership is an invitation to put your spiritual values into action by supporting our shared commitment to service while deepening your study and practice in the living Himalayan Tradition.

The Secret of the Yoga Sutra
Samadhi Pada
Pandit Rajmani Tigunait, PhD

The Yoga Sutra is the living source wisdom of the yoga tradition, and is as relevant today as it was 2,200 years ago when it was codified by the sage Patanjali. Using this ancient yogic text as a guide, we can unlock the hidden power of yoga, and experience the promise of yoga in our lives. By applying its living wisdom in our practice, we can achieve the purpose of life: lasting fulfillment and ultimate freedom.

Paperback, 6" x 9", 331 pages
$24.95, ISBN 978-0-89389-277-7

The Practice of the Yoga Sutra
Sadhana Pada
Pandit Rajmani Tigunait, PhD

In Pandit Tigunait's practitioner-oriented commentary series, we see this ancient text through the filter of scholarly understanding and experiential knowledge gained through decades of advanced yogic practices. Through *The Secret of the Yoga Sutra* and *The Practice of the Yoga Sutra*, we receive the gift of living wisdom he received from the masters of the Himalayan Tradition, leading us to lasting happiness.

Paperback, 6" x 9", 389 Pages
$24.95, ISBN 978-0-89389-279-1

To order: 800-822-4547
Email: mailorder@HimalayanInstitute.org
Visit: HimalayanInstitute.org

HIMALAYAN
INSTITUTE®

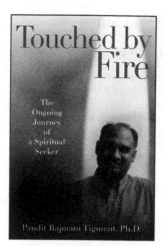

Touched by Fire
Pandit Rajmani Tigunait, PhD

This vivid autobiography of a remarkable spiritual leader—Pandit Rajmani Tigunait, PhD—reveals his experiences and encounters with numerous teachers, sages, and his master, the late Swami Rama of the Himalayas. His well-told journey is filled with years of disciplined study and the struggle to master the lessons and skills passed to him. *Touched by Fire* brings Western culture a glimpse of Eastern philosophies in a clear, understandable fashion, and provides numerous photographs showing a part of the world many will never see for themselves.

Paperback with flaps, 6" x 9", 296 pages
$16.95, ISBN 978-0-89389-239-5

At the Eleventh Hour
Pandit Rajmani Tigunait, PhD

This book is more than the biography of a great sage—it is a revelation of the many astonishing accomplishments Swami Rama achieved in his life. These pages serve as a guide to the more esoteric and advanced practices of yoga and tantra not commonly taught or understood in the West. And they bring you to holy places in India, revealing why these sacred sites are important and how to go about visiting them. The wisdom in these stories penetrates beyond the power of words.

Paperback with flaps, 6" x 9", 448 pages
$18.95, ISBN 978-0-89389-211-1

To order: 800-822-4547
Email: mailorder@HimalayanInstitute.org
Visit: HimalayanInstitute.org

HIMALAYAN
INSTITUTE®

From Death to Birth
Pandit Rajmani Tigunait, PhD

From Death to Birth takes us along the soul's journey from death to birth, dispelling the frequent misconceptions about this subject by revealing little-known but powerful truths. Through a series of lively stories drawn from the ancient scriptures and his own experience, Pandit Tigunait reveals what karma really is, how we can create it, why it becomes our destiny, and how we can use it to shape the future of our dreams.

Paperback, 6" x 9", 216 pages
$15.95, ISBN 978-0-89389-147-3

Sakti Sadhana
Pandit Rajmani Tigunait, PhD

The knowledge that enlightens the aspiring student into the mystery of life here and hereafter is the *Tripura Rahasya*. This text is one of the most significant scriptures in the tradition of tantra yoga. Its beauty lies in the fact that it expounds the lofty knowledge of inner truth while systematically offering practical instructions on *sakti sadhana*—the task of awakening the dormant fire within and leading it to higher awareness, or the highest chakra.

Paperback, 6" x 9", 196 pages
$10.95, ISBN 978-0-89389-140-4

To order: 800-822-4547
Email: mailorder@HimalayanInstitute.org
Visit: HimalayanInstitute.org

HIMALAYAN
INSTITUTE®

Tantra Unveiled
Pandit Rajmani Tigunait, PhD

This powerful book describes authentic tantra, what distinguishes it from other spiritual paths, and how the tantric way combines hatha yoga, meditation, visualization, ayurveda, and other disciplines. Taking us back to ancient times, Pandit Tigunait shares his experiences with tantric masters and the techniques they taught him. *Tantra Unveiled* is most valuable for those who wish to live the essence of tantra—practicing spirituality while experiencing a rich outer life.

Paperback, 6" x 9", 152 pages
$14.95, ISBN 978-0-89389-158-9

Moving Inward
Rolf Sovik, PsyD

Rolf Sovik shows readers of all levels how to transition from asanas to meditation. Combining practical advice on breathing and relaxation with timeless asana postures, he systematically guides us through the process. This book provides a five-stage plan to basic meditation, step-by-step guidelines for perfect postures, and six methods for training the breath. Both the novice and the advanced student will benefit from Sovik's startling insights into the mystery of meditation.

Paperback, 6" x 9", 197 pages
$14.95, ISBN 978-0-89389-247-0